JOE GILBERT

The Growth Anthology

50 Books That Redefined Self Mastery

Contents

1

Embarking on a Voyage of Self-Discovery: Navigating the World of Self-Help

In every corner of the world, across all cultures and societies, there lies an innate human desire to grow, to understand oneself better, and to find a deeper sense of purpose and fulfillment. This shared quest for personal growth and the timeless search for wisdom has given birth to a vast and varied genre: self-help. Through the annals of time, thinkers, scholars, researchers, and storytellers have sought to capture the essence of human potential, and to guide us towards realizing it.

But with such a plethora of voices and perspectives, where does one begin? How does one sift through the vast sea of knowledge to find the insights that truly resonate?

A Curated Journey

This book aims to be your compass. We've distilled the wisdom from fifty of the most impactful self-help books ever penned, offering you a curated journey through the insights and techniques that have transformed lives and shaped the way we think about self-improvement.

The Universality of Core Themes

As you navigate these summaries, you'll uncover a fascinating tapestry of ideas. Yet, amidst the diversity, you'll also discover common threads — universal truths and principles that echo across cultures and eras. Themes like the power of perseverance, the importance of authenticity, and the deep-seated human need for connection recur, serving as reminders of our shared human experience.

Why Begin This Journey?

- **Condensed Wisdom**: We live in an age of information overload. This book provides a distilled essence, capturing the core tenets and transformative ideas of each selected work.
- **A Starting Point**: Think of this as a sampler, an appetizer. While these summaries provide valuable insights, they're also an invitation to delve deeper into books that resonate with you.
- **Personalized Insights**: Every reader is unique, and so will be their takeaways. What resonates deeply with one person might differ for another. This journey offers the opportunity for myriad personalized epiphanies.

Setting Sail

Before we embark on this journey, a gentle reminder: personal growth isn't about a destination. It's about the journey itself, the continual process of learning, unlearning, and evolving. It's about the introspection and the outward exploration, the challenges and the triumphs.

And so, as we set sail through the vast oceans of self-help literature, remember that every insight, every piece of wisdom, is a tool. How you use it, adapt it, and integrate it into your life's unique tapestry is the true essence of self-help.

"The only journey is the one within." — Rainer Maria Rilke

With that, let's turn the page and begin our expedition into the transformative world of self-help.

2

"Think and Grow Rich" by Napoleon Hill

Napoleon Hill's "Think and Grow Rich" is a classic in the personal development genre, written in 1937 during the aftermath of the Great Depression. It emerged from Hill's study of the habits and mindsets of the most successful people of his time. The book doesn't just focus on the accumulation of monetary wealth but also on success in its broadest sense.

Key Concepts:

1. **Desire:** To achieve a goal, you must have an intense, burning desire for it. Without this fervor, achieving your goal becomes difficult. Hill suggests writing down the amount of money you desire, what you're willing to give in return, and a definite date by which you'll achieve it.

2. **Faith:** You must believe and have faith that you will achieve your goal. Hill stresses the power of autosuggestion: the principle that when beliefs are repeated and emotionalized, they're imprinted into the subconscious

mind and then materialize into reality.

3. **Autosuggestion:** This is the repeated self-affirmation of your goals. By regularly reinforcing your ambitions to your subconscious mind, you can influence it to assist in achieving those aims.

4. **Specialized Knowledge:** General knowledge, by itself, won't lead to success. Hill encourages readers to focus on specialized knowledge relevant to their goals.

5. **Imagination:** All achievements and riches begin as an idea. Use creative imagination to come up with innovative solutions and new ideas.

6. **Organized Planning:** This involves arranging definite steps towards your goal and executing them. Without a clear plan, it's difficult to realize your ambitions.

7. **Decision:** Hill observed that successful people make decisions quickly and change them slowly, while unsuccessful people do the opposite.

8. **Persistence:** Persistence is key to overcoming failures and obstacles. Most people give up just before they're about to succeed.

9. **Power of the Master Mind:** Surround yourself with a group of like-minded individuals who can help you achieve your goals. The combined energies of this group can elevate each member's potential.

10. **The Mystery of Sex Transmutation:** Hill touches upon the concept of redirecting sexual energy into activities that further one's goal for success, arguing that sexual drive is one of the most potent human energies.

11. **The Subconscious Mind:** This chapter emphasizes the importance of controlling thoughts to influence the subconscious mind positively.

12. **The Brain:** The human brain can be likened to a broadcasting and receiving station for thoughts. By harnessing its power, one can achieve great things.
13. **The Sixth Sense:** This refers to the creative imagination, where hunches and inspirations come from. It's the point at which the mind contacts sources of knowledge not available through the ordinary rate of perception.

Fear: Hill identifies six basic fears: fear of poverty, criticism, ill health, loss of love, old age, and death. Recognizing and addressing these fears is essential for success.

Why "Think and Grow Rich" is a Classic and Its Importance:

- **Universal Principles:** Hill's teachings are based on universal principles of success, which means they are applicable in multiple areas of life and not just monetary wealth.
- **Historical Context:** Given that the book was written during the Great Depression, its advice provided hope and actionable steps to many during challenging times.
- **Depth of Research:** Hill spent over 20 years researching and interviewing successful individuals, making the book a compilation of rich insights.
- **Mental Aspect:** The book emphasizes the power of thought, making readers realize that mindset is a significant precursor to action and success.

Why I've added this book to my list

"Think and Grow Rich" is included in the list of greatest self-development books because of its lasting impact, universal principles, and practical guidelines that have helped millions to achieve success. Hill's work has set the foundation for many modern personal development books, making it a cornerstone in the genre.

Overall, Napoleon Hill's "Think and Grow Rich" is more than just a guide to amassing wealth. It offers readers a roadmap to self-discovery, personal development, and the attainment of their dreams, making it a masterpiece in the self-help domain.

3

"How to Win Friends and Influence People" by Dale Carnegie

Published in 1936, Dale Carnegie's "How to Win Friends and Influence People" remains one of the best-selling books of all time. Carnegie's advice revolves around maximizing personal interactions, fostering positive relationships, and building influence. The teachings are rooted in the importance of genuine interest in others, understanding human nature, and the power of positive reinforcement.

Key Concepts:

Fundamental Techniques in Handling People:

- **Avoid Criticism, Condemnation, or Complaint:** Negative feedback often results in resentment.
- **Give Honest and Sincere Appreciation:** Authentic compliments motivate and uplift people.
- **Arouse in the Other Person an Eager Want:** Understand the

needs and desires of others to influence them effectively.

Six Ways to Make People Like You:

- **Become Genuinely Interested in Other People:** Authentic interest fosters connection.
- **Smile:** A simple yet impactful gesture that attracts positivity.
- **Remember People's Names:** A person's name is, to them, the sweetest sound.
- **Be a Good Listener and Encourage Others to Talk About Themselves:** This showcases genuine interest and makes others feel valued.
- **Talk in Terms of the Other Person's Interests:** It builds rapport and understanding.
- **Make the Other Person Feel Important and Do It Sincerely:** Recognizing and affirming the value in others builds trust and goodwill.

How to Win People to Your Way of Thinking:

- **Avoid Arguments:** They rarely result in genuine agreement and often lead to resentment.
- **Show Respect for the Other Person's Opinions:** Avoid saying "you're wrong."
- **Admit Faults Quickly and Emphatically:** It disarms opposition.
- **Begin Conversations in a Friendly Way:** It sets a positive tone for any interaction.
- **Get the Other Person Saying "Yes, Yes" Immediately:** This creates a positive momentum.

- **Let the Other Person Do Most of the Talking:** It gives them a sense of importance.
- **Let Others Feel the Idea Is Theirs:** It creates personal investment in the idea.
- **Try Honestly to See Things from the Other Person's Point of View:** Empathy builds understanding.
- **Be Sympathetic to Others' Ideas and Desires:** Genuine sympathy can build rapport.
- **Appeal to Nobler Motives:** Elevate the conversation and the motives.
- **Dramatize Your Ideas:** Make your ideas compelling and relatable.
- **Throw Down a Challenge:** Challenge others in a way that inspires and motivates them.

Be a Leader – How to Change People Without Giving Offense or Arousing Resentment:

- **Begin with Praise and Honest Appreciation:** It sets a positive tone.
- **Call Attention to People's Mistakes Indirectly:** This reduces defensiveness.
- **Talk About Your Mistakes Before Criticizing the Other Person:** It shows humility.
- **Ask Questions Instead of Giving Direct Orders:** It encourages collaboration.
- **Let the Other Person Save Face:** Preserve dignity.
- **Praise Every Improvement:** Positive reinforcement works wonders.
- **Give the Other Person a Fine Reputation to Live Up To:** Elevate their self-perception.

- **Encourage and Make the Fault Seem Easy to Correct:** It boosts confidence.
- **Make the Other Person Happy About Doing What You Suggest:** It creates willingness and enthusiasm.

Why "How to Win Friends and Influence People" is a Classic and Its Importance:

- **Universality:** The book's principles apply to almost every human interaction, making it relevant across generations.
- **Human-Centric:** Carnegie's teachings are rooted in understanding and valuing human nature.
- **Practicality:** The book provides actionable advice, making it easy for readers to apply the teachings in real-life scenarios.

Inclusion in this book:

The inclusion of "How to Win Friends and Influence People" in the list of greatest self-development books is a testament to its timeless teachings. Carnegie's emphasis on genuine human connections, the importance of empathy, and the art of positive influence has impacted millions, making it an essential read for anyone seeking personal and professional growth.

4

"The 7 Habits of Highly Effective People" by Stephen R. Covey

Stephen R. Covey's "The 7 Habits of Highly Effective People", first published in 1989, is a holistic approach to personal and interpersonal effectiveness. Rather than offering quick fixes, Covey provides enduring habits for long-term success. These habits are based on principles and are aimed at helping individuals create a balanced, fulfilling life.

The 7 Habits:

Be Proactive (Personal Responsibility):

· This habit is about recognizing that our actions are a result of our choices, not our conditions. We can choose our reactions to any given situation, emphasizing the power of individual initiative to change circumstances.

Begin with the End in Mind (Vision):

· Define a clear understanding of what you want to achieve in the long run. This habit underscores the importance of goal-setting and having a mission for your life.

Put First Things First (Prioritization):

· Focus on what's important, not just urgent. This habit encourages managing time and tasks based on priorities, emphasizing the significance of discipline and organization in achieving important goals.

Think Win-Win (Mutual Benefit):

· Cultivate an abundance mindset, seeking mutual benefit in all interactions. This habit is about creating scenarios where all parties involved can benefit, rather than approaching interactions as zero-sum competitions.

Seek First to Understand, Then to Be Understood (Empathetic Communication):

· Before offering advice or solutions, strive to understand deeply. This habit stresses the importance of active listening and empathy in communications.

Synergize (Collaborative Teamwork):

· Recognize the strength in working collaboratively with others to achieve goals. This habit emphasizes that the whole is greater than the sum of its parts and that cooperation often leads to better results than individual efforts.

Sharpen the Saw (Self-Renewal):

- Regularly renew and improve oneself in the physical, mental, emotional, and spiritual domains. This habit is about self-care and continuous learning, ensuring longevity and resilience.

Why "The 7 Habits of Highly Effective People" is a Classic and Its Importance:

- **Holistic Approach:** The book doesn't just address professional success but touches on personal growth and interpersonal relationships, providing a comprehensive framework for overall effectiveness.
- **Foundation on Principles:** Covey's habits are based on timeless principles, making them enduring and universally applicable.
- **Actionable Framework:** The 7 habits provide a clear, actionable framework that readers can follow to improve various aspects of their lives.

Inclusion in this book

"The 7 Habits of Highly Effective People" has been included in the list of greatest self-development books due to its profound impact on personal growth and leadership over the decades.

Its principles-based approach has inspired millions to achieve personal mastery and effective interpersonal relationships, making it a staple in personal development literature.

5

"Man's Search for Meaning" by Viktor E. Frankl

"Man's Search for Meaning" is a powerful memoir and psychological exploration penned by Viktor E. Frankl, a neurologist, psychiatrist, and Holocaust survivor. Published in 1946, the book gives a riveting account of Frankl's experiences in Nazi concentration camps, while also introducing his psychotherapeutic method which emphasizes the importance of finding meaning in all forms of existence.

Key Takeaways:

Life in Nazi Concentration Camps:

- The book starts with Frankl's personal experiences during his time in four Nazi concentration camps, including Auschwitz. He details the horrors and human degradation witnessed, but also moments of hope, kindness, and resilience.

Logotherapy – Finding Meaning:

- Frankl introduces his therapeutic approach known as "logotherapy". While traditional psychotherapy places emphasis on the will to pleasure (Freud) or power (Adler), logotherapy focuses on the will to meaning. Frankl argues that the primary human drive is to discover a sense of purpose and meaning in life.

Three Paths to Meaning:

- Frankl suggests there are three primary ways to find meaning:

1. **Through work or doing a deed.**
2. **By experiencing something or encountering someone.**
3. **Through the attitude we adopt toward unavoidable suffering.**

Freedom to Choose One's Attitude:

- Despite facing extreme conditions in the concentration camps, Frankl discovered that inmates had the freedom to choose their attitude towards their suffering. This understanding that one can always choose how to respond is central to logotherapy.

Existential Vacuum:

- Frankl mentions a widespread phenomenon in the 20th century that he terms the "existential vacuum", a feeling of emptiness and meaninglessness. He contends that many psychological issues arise from this vacuum.

Future Orientation:

- A significant element of logotherapy is its future orientation. It stresses that one should not look to the past for meaning but instead to the tasks and responsibilities that await them.

Why "Man's Search for Meaning" is a Classic and Its Importance:

- **Human Resilience:** The memoir showcases the incredible resilience of the human spirit, even in the face of unimaginable adversity.
- **Universal Quest for Meaning:** Frankl's exploration of life's meaning and purpose is a universal quest, resonating with readers from diverse backgrounds and life situations.
- **Existential Exploration:** The book delves deep into existentialism, encouraging readers to reflect on their lives and the broader questions of existence.

Inclusion in this book:

"Man's Search for Meaning" finds its place in the list of greatest self-development books because of its profound impact on readers worldwide. Through a combination of harrowing memoir and insightful psychology, Frankl provides a perspective on life's challenges and the enduring human quest for meaning. It's a timeless piece that offers hope, resilience, and a deeper understanding of oneself.

6

"Atomic Habits: An Easy & Proven Way to Build Good Habits & Break Bad Ones" by James Clear

James Clear's "Atomic Habits" provides a comprehensive guide to habit formation, illustrating how small changes can lead to remarkable results. The title emphasizes the idea of "atomic" changes: tiny adjustments that, over time, create significant outcomes.

Key Concepts:

The Compound Effect of Habits:

- Just as money multiplies through compound interest, the effects of habits compound over time. Small improvements can add up to produce significant positive changes in the long run.

The Habit Loop – Cue, Craving, Response, Reward:

- Clear breaks down the habitual process into four stages: cue (trigger), craving (desire to change state), response (actual habit), and reward (end result of the habit). Understanding this loop is crucial for creating or breaking habits.

The Four Laws of Behavior Change:

- To create a good habit, Clear proposes four laws linked with the habit loop:

1. **Make it Obvious (Cue)**: Design an environment that presents clear triggers for your habits.
2. **Make it Attractive (Craving)**: Use temptation bundling or associate habits with positive feelings.
3. **Make it Easy (Response)**: Reduce friction to make the habit action as easy as possible.
4. **Make it Satisfying (Reward)**: Give yourself an immediate reward to make the habit stick.

For breaking bad habits, you simply invert these laws.

Habit Stacking:

- Build on your current habits by "stacking" a new habit on top of an existing one. The formula is: "After [current habit], I will [new habit]."

Identity-Based Habits:

- Focus on who you wish to become, not what you want to achieve. By changing your identity (e.g., "I'm a runner" instead of "I run"), you anchor new habits more deeply.

Environment and Habits:

- Your environment plays a significant role in determining which habits stick and which don't. Design your environment to make desirable habits more accessible and undesirable habits harder to engage in.

The Two-Minute Rule:

- When starting a new habit, it should take less than two minutes to do. This concept simplifies complex habits into easy starting points, making it easier to initiate them.

Why "Atomic Habits" is Significant and Its Importance:

- **Practicality:** Clear offers actionable strategies, making it easy for readers to implement the ideas in real-life scenarios.
- **Holistic Approach:** Rather than focusing solely on outcomes, Clear emphasizes the importance of systems and processes.
- **Identity Transformation:** The book's emphasis on identity-based habits offers a fresh perspective on habit formation, making it more sustainable.

Inclusion in this book:

"Atomic Habits" has been included in the list of greatest self-development books due to its deep insights into the mechanics of habits and its potential to drive transformative change. James Clear's blend of scientific research, engaging storytelling, and practical advice offers readers an accessible and effective path to personal growth.

7

"The Power of Now: A Guide to Spiritual Enlightenment" by Eckhart Tolle

In "The Power of Now", Eckhart Tolle introduces readers to the concept of living in the present moment as a pathway to spiritual enlightenment. Drawing from his personal transformation, Tolle explores the nature of the mind, the source of true peace, and the liberation from the tyranny of compulsive thinking.

Main Themes:

Living in the Present:

- Tolle emphasizes the significance of living fully in the present moment, or the "Now". According to him, the present is the only reality, and by anchoring ourselves in it, we can find genuine peace and happiness.

Ego and Identity:

· The ego, as Tolle describes, is a false self created by un-
conscious identification with the mind. This identification
creates a false narrative of who we are, leading to suffering.
Enlightenment is realizing that our true self is beyond the
ego and mind.

Pain-Body:

· Tolle introduces the concept of the "pain-body", an accu-
mulated energy resulting from past traumas and emotional
pain. This energy feeds on negative thoughts and experiences. By recognizing and observing the pain-body without
judgment, we can dissolve it.

Freedom from Thought:

· One of the primary messages of the book is that we are
not our thoughts. By observing our thoughts without
attachment, we can free ourselves from their grip and
connect with a deeper sense of self.

Surrender:

· Surrendering doesn't mean giving up but refers to the
act of accepting the present moment without resistance.
By surrendering to what is, we can find peace even in
challenging situations.

Portal to the Now:

· Tolle suggests various techniques to access the present moment, such as observing one's breath, immersing in nature, and embracing silence.

Why "The Power of Now" is Significant:

· **Transformative Ideas:** Tolle's insights into the nature of mind, ego, and reality offer readers a new perspective on life and the nature of suffering.
· **Accessible Spirituality:** Tolle presents profound spiritual concepts in a manner that's accessible to modern readers, irrespective of their religious background.
· **Practical Guidance:** The book offers practical techniques to practice presence and find peace in daily life.

Inclusion in this book:

"The Power of Now" is included in the list of greatest self-development books due to its profound impact on readers worldwide. Its message of presence, acceptance, and inner peace has resonated with millions, offering a fresh perspective on spirituality and the quest for happiness. The book's influence extends across various spheres, including personal development, spirituality, and psychology.

8

"Awaken the Giant Within: How to Take Immediate Control of Your Mental, Emotional, Physical and Financial Destiny!"

Tony Robbins, a renowned life coach, and motivational speaker offers a comprehensive guide to self-mastery in "Awaken the Giant Within". In this book, Robbins shares strategies and techniques for mastering your emotions, body, relationships, finances, and life.

Key Insights:

Personal Change and Decisions:

- Robbins emphasizes that decisions, not conditions, determine our destiny. Making true decisions means committing to achieving results and cutting off any other possibility.

Pain and Pleasure Principle:

- According to Robbins, all human behavior is driven by the need to avoid pain and the desire to gain pleasure. By associating pain with unwanted behaviors and pleasure with desired ones, you can reprogram your motivations.

Belief Systems:

- Our beliefs about what we are and what we can be precisely determine what we can be. By challenging and reshaping limiting beliefs, one can expand their potential.

Neuro-Associative Conditioning (NAC):

- Robbins introduces the concept of NAC, which is a process of reconditioning the brain to associate pain or pleasure with certain behaviors, thereby facilitating change.

The Power of Questions:

- The questions we consistently ask ourselves determine our focus, and thus, how we feel and act. By asking empowering questions, we can shift our focus and transform our emotions and experiences.

The Six Human Needs:

- Robbins identifies six fundamental human needs: certainty, uncertainty/variety, significance, connection/love, growth, and contribution. The way individuals prioritize these needs shapes their lives and behaviors.

Mastering Finances:

- Robbins provides insights and strategies for taking control of one's financial destiny, emphasizing the importance of making informed decisions, seeking knowledge, and taking calculated risks.

Emotional Mastery:

- To achieve emotional mastery, one must understand the underlying patterns that evoke emotional responses and learn how to change them.

Building Strong Relationships:

- Robbins stresses the importance of communication, under-standing, and flexibility in building and maintaining strong relationships.

Significance and Importance of the Book:

- **Holistic Approach:** Robbins offers a holistic approach to personal development, addressing various aspects of life, from emotions to finances.
- **Action-Oriented:** The book emphasizes taking immediate action. Robbins consistently pushes readers to apply the principles and make tangible changes in their lives.

- **Broad Impact:** "Awaken the Giant Within" has influenced countless individuals in their personal and professional lives, making it a staple in the realm of personal development literature.

Inclusion in this book:

Tony Robbins' "Awaken the Giant Within" is a comprehensive guide that spans a range of topics, from fundamental psychological principles to actionable financial strategies. Robbins' ability to distill complex concepts into accessible, actionable insights has made this book a classic in the self-help genre. Its enduring popularity and impact on readers globally underscore its significance in personal development literature.

9

"Daring Greatly: How the Courage to Be Vulnerable Transforms the Way We Live, Love, Parent, and Lead" by Brené Brown

Brené Brown, a research professor and renowned expert on vulnerability, courage, worthiness, and shame, dives deep into the concept of vulnerability in "Daring Greatly." She posits that embracing vulnerability is not a sign of weakness but a source of strength, leading to more meaningful connections, creativity, and joy.

Principal Insights:

Vulnerability is Strength:

- Contrary to the prevalent belief that vulnerability is a sign of weakness, Brown argues it's the most accurate measure of courage. Vulnerability is the birthplace of innovation, creativity, and change.

Shame and Vulnerability:

- Brown discusses how shame, the fear of disconnection due to perceived unworthiness, is a barrier to vulnerability. By recognizing and combating shame, we can embrace vulnerability and connect authentically.

Scarcity Mindset:

- Living in a culture of "never enough" (never good enough, successful enough, thin enough, etc.) makes it hard for people to feel worthy of love and belonging. Overcoming this scarcity mindset is essential for embracing vulnerability.

Wholehearted Living:

- Brown introduces the concept of "Wholehearted Living" – a way of engaging with the world from a place of worthiness, involving courage, compassion, and connection.

Parenting and Vulnerability:

- Embracing vulnerability is pivotal in parenting. By being vulnerable, parents can model authenticity, resilience, and self-worth for their children.

Vulnerability in Leadership:

- Brown highlights that vulnerability is crucial in leadership.

It fosters trust, collaboration, and innovation within teams and organizations.

Strategies to Embrace Vulnerability:

· Brown provides actionable insights and strategies to embrace vulnerability, like understanding and managing shame, practicing gratitude, and cultivating a resilient spirit.

Why "Daring Greatly" is Important:

· **Paradigm Shift:** Brown's work shifts the perspective on vulnerability, challenging societal norms and presenting vulnerability as a source of power.
· **Research-Based:** Unlike many self-help books, "Daring Greatly" is rooted in extensive research, lending credibility to its claims and insights.
· **Universal Relevance:** The themes of vulnerability, shame, and worthiness are universally relevant, making the book resonate with a broad audience.

Inclusion in this book:

"Daring Greatly" is a transformative exploration of the human experience, shedding light on the power of vulnerability in various spheres of life - from personal relationships to leadership. Brené Brown's unique blend of deep research, relatable storytelling, and actionable insights has made the book a standout in the self-development genre. Its impact on personal growth, leadership paradigms, and parenting perspectives underscores its importance in the literature of personal development.

10

"The Power of Habit: Why We Do What We Do in Life and Business" by Charles Duhigg

11

"Rich Dad Poor Dad" by Robert T. Kiyosaki

"Rich Dad Poor Dad" is Robert T. Kiyosaki's personal journey into financial understanding, presented through the contrasting advice of two father figures. One, his biological father (referred to as "Poor Dad"), emphasizes traditional education and a steady job. The other, the father of a childhood friend (referred to as "Rich Dad"), offers insights into wealth-building and financial independence.

The Importance of Financial Literacy:

- Kiyosaki stresses the significance of understanding finances, including the ability to read and understand financial statements. Being financially literate is key to making informed decisions about money.

Assets vs. Liabilities:

- One of the book's core principles is the distinction between assets and liabilities. In Kiyosaki's terms, assets put money into your pocket, and liabilities take money out. The wealthy buy assets, while the poor and middle class often accumulate liabilities thinking they are assets.

The Rat Race:

- Kiyosaki describes how many people get caught in a cycle of working for money instead of having money work for them. By prioritizing high salaries, promotions, and job security, they increase their expenses with each raise, perpetuating a cycle of working to support their lifestyle.

Importance of Entrepreneurship:

- Rather than relying solely on a traditional job and salary, Kiyosaki champions entrepreneurship and investing as paths to financial independence. He emphasizes the need to take calculated risks and learn from failures.

Overcoming Fear and Laziness:

- Fear of losing money and laziness are two significant barriers to financial success, according to Kiyosaki. Overcoming these barriers by seeking knowledge and taking action is essential.

The Value of Experience:

- Kiyosaki suggests that real-life experience is a more effective teacher than traditional education when it comes to financial matters. Mistakes are opportunities to learn.

Seeking Opportunities:

- The rich don't wait for opportunities to come to them; they actively seek and create them. Investing in real estate, building businesses, and leveraging market opportunities are ways the wealthy build their assets.

Inclusion in this book:

"Rich Dad Poor Dad" has been lauded for its approach to financial education, particularly its emphasis on financial independence and building wealth through investing in assets. Kiyosaki's lessons, derived from the contrasting advice of his two "dads," challenge conventional beliefs about money, work, and life. While some critics argue that the book oversimplifies complex financial strategies and lacks detailed actionable steps, its principles have resonated with many seeking an alternative perspective on money and investing.

12

"Tools of Titans" by Tim Ferriss

"Tools of Titans" is a compilation of lessons and insights Tim Ferriss gathered from interviewing more than 200 world-class performers on his podcast, "The Tim Ferriss Show". The book is structured in three main sections, reflecting Ben Franklin's famous quote: "Early to bed and early to rise, makes a man healthy, wealthy, and wise."

Healthy:

- In this section, Ferriss explores the habits, routines, and strategies the Titans use to maintain their physical and mental health. Topics range from exercise routines, sleep habits, meditation techniques, and even dietary practices.
- **Key Insights:**
- Many successful individuals prioritize meditation or mindfulness practices.
- The importance of a regular sleep schedule and optimal sleep environment.
- The benefits of various types of diets and fasting protocols.

Wealthy:

- This portion dives into the practices and principles that the interviewed subjects attribute to their financial and career success.

Key Insights:

- The value of creating automated income streams.
- The importance of negotiation skills.
- Approaches to investing, both in terms of money and time.
- Lessons on entrepreneurship, including the significance of taking calculated risks.

Wise:

- Ferriss delves into the philosophical, spiritual, and intellectual frameworks that guide the lives of the Titans.

Key Insights:

- The recurrent theme of stoicism and the value of focusing on factors within one's control.
- The power of journaling as a means of reflection and clarity.
- Emphasis on lifelong learning and continuous self-improvement.

Throughout the book, Ferriss punctuates the insights from his interviewees with his own experiences and commentary, providing context and personal anecdotes.

Notable Figures Featured: The book showcases a diverse range of individuals, from tech moguls like Peter Thiel and Marc Andreessen to creatives like Maria Popova and Malcolm Gladwell, and from athletes like Arnold Schwarzenegger to meditation experts like Sam Harris.

Inclusion in this book:

"Tools of Titans" offers readers a unique opportunity to peek into the lives and minds of some of the most successful and accomplished individuals across various fields. Its format, broken down into bite-sized yet profound insights, makes it a valuable reference that one can revisit multiple times. The book underscores that while there's no single path to success, certain habits, mindsets, and strategies are recurrent among those who achieve greatness.

13

"Start with Why" by Simon Sinek

"Start with Why" presents the idea that successful individuals and organizations are those that have a clear understanding of their "Why" – their purpose, cause, or belief that drives them. Simon Sinek posits that understanding this "Why" is what allows these entities to inspire others and achieve remarkable things.

The Golden Circle:

- **Definition:** A model developed by Sinek, composed of three concentric circles: the innermost is "Why," followed by "How," and the outermost is "What."
- **Core Idea:** Most organizations can articulate "What" they do and "How" they do it, but very few can articulate "Why" they do what they do. The most inspiring leaders and organizations, however, start with a clear understanding of their "Why."

Why is Not About Money:

- **Definition:** "Why" is not a profit. It's a purpose, cause, or belief.
- **Core Idea:** While making money is essential for the vitality and sustainability of a business, it's not the reason a business exists. Money is a result.

The Biology of the Golden Circle:

- **Definition:** The Golden Circle aligns with the three major levels of the brain, corresponding to the decision-making process.
- **Core Idea:** The limbic brain, which is responsible for feelings like trust and loyalty, aligns with the "Why." It's where decision-making happens. This is why appealing to people's emotions (i.e., their "Why") is so effective.

Manipulation vs. Inspiration:

- **Definition:** Manipulations (e.g., price reductions, promotions) are ways to generate a transaction or behavior without building loyalty. Inspiration is the ability to mobilize people towards a shared vision.
- **Core Idea:** While manipulations can drive short-term results, they don't foster loyalty or a lasting connection. Starting with "Why" leads to inspiration and long-term loyalty.

The Diffusion of Innovations:

- **Definition:** An idea conceptualized by Everett Rogers that classifies people into categories based on their adoption of innovations: Innovators, Early Adopters, Early Majority, Late Majority, and Laggards.

- **Core Idea:** Those who start with "Why" are able to attract the early adopters and achieve market success that then cascades to broader populations.

Clarity, Discipline, and Consistency:

- **Definition:** The three things needed to harness the power of "Why."
- **Core Idea:** Leaders and organizations must be clear about their "Why," be disciplined in how they bring it to life, and be consistent in what they do and say.

Why "Start with Why" is a Thought-Provoking Guide for Leaders:

Simon Sinek's "Start with Why" is a rallying cry for those aiming to inspire others and create lasting change. By diving into the core essence of inspiration and its role in leadership and innovation, the book challenges the status quo of business thinking. Through a blend of compelling anecdotes and well-researched insights, Sinek offers a blueprint for leaders to build more meaningful and sustainable organizations. It's not just about tactics or strategies; it's about tapping into the very core of human behavior and motivation.

14

"Who Moved My Cheese?" by Dr. Spencer Johnson

"Who Moved My Cheese?" is a motivational business fable that explores how different individuals deal with change in their personal and professional lives. The narrative is set in a maze, where four characters search for "cheese" that represents happiness, success, or whatever one desires in life.

The Characters:

- **Sniff:** Detects change early and quickly adapts to it. He sniffs out the situation and anticipates when he needs to move with the cheese.
- **Scurry:** Doesn't overthink or overanalyze—when change happens, he quickly scurries into action.
- **Hem:** Dislikes change and fears the unknown. He resists change and wishes for things to return to how they were.
- **Haw:** Initially hesitant about change, but he learns to embrace it over time. He understands that moving with the cheese leads to new opportunities.

The Story:

Initially, all characters enjoy a constant supply of cheese. But one day, the cheese is moved. Sniff and Scurry quickly move on to find new cheese, while Hem and Haw stay behind, upset about the change and hoping the cheese will return. Over time, Haw realizes the need to move on and starts looking for new cheese, while Hem remains resistant and stuck in his ways.

Key Lessons:

- **Anticipate Change:** Be prepared for the cheese to move, as change is a natural part of life.
- **Adapt to Change Quickly:** The quicker you let go of the old cheese (old ways or past success), the sooner you can enjoy the new.
- **Enjoy Change:** Embrace the adventure of finding new cheese.
- **Be Ready to Change Again and Again:** Keep moving with the cheese and stay agile.

The Cheese and Maze Metaphors:

The cheese can represent anything one aspires for—be it a job, relationship, money, or recognition. The maze represents the environment or the challenges one navigates in pursuit of the cheese.

Why "Who Moved My Cheese?" is a Noteworthy Read for Anyone Facing Change:

Dr. Spencer Johnson's fable has gained worldwide acclaim for its universal message about life's inevitability: change. The book serves as a simple, yet profound, guide for dealing with change positively. Its lessons resonate with individuals and organizations alike, as everyone faces change—whether by choice or circumstance. The allegory encourages a proactive mindset, adaptability, and the willingness to leave one's comfort zone.

15

"The Life-Changing Magic of Tidying Up" by Marie Kondo

"The Life-Changing Magic of Tidying Up" is a best-selling guide to decluttering and organizing your living space written by Japanese cleaning consultant Marie Kondo. Here's a summary:

The KonMari Method:

At the heart of the book is the "KonMari Method," a unique approach to decluttering that departs from traditional advice. Instead of decluttering room by room or little by little, Kondo suggests decluttering by category and doing it all at once, in a short span of time. This radical tidying festival is supposed to be a one-time event that results in permanent change.

Key Principles:

1. **Tidy All at Once:** By making tidying a special event, you change your mindset and can keep the clutter from coming back.
2. **Visualize the Life You Want:** Before you start, think deeply about why you want to tidy and how you envision your ideal life.
3. **Determine if It 'Sparks Joy':** Hold each item, and if it doesn't bring you joy or is not necessary, thank it for its service and let it go. This gratitude makes parting with items less painful.
4. **Tidy by Category:** Start with clothes, then books, papers, miscellaneous items (komono), and lastly sentimental items. By the time you get to sentimental items, your decision-making skills will have improved.
5. **Designate a Place for Everything:** After decluttering, the next step is to ensure that every item has a designated place. This prevents the rebound effect where clutter can accumulate again.

Details of the Process:

- **Clothes:** Begin with your clothes. Lay them all out, touch each one, and decide if it sparks joy. Kondo suggests folding clothes in a particular way to stand them upright, which makes storage more efficient and items easier to find.
- **Books:** Like clothes, lay all your books out. Only keep the ones that spark joy or will be read in the future.
- **Papers:** Most papers can be discarded, but those that are necessary should be sorted into: needs attention, should

be kept short-term, and should be kept indefinitely.

- **Komono (Miscellaneous):** This is a broad category, encompassing everything from kitchen goods to bathroom supplies. The key is to break it down into smaller subcategories and tackle one at a time.
- **Sentimental Items:** By this point, you'll be better at knowing what truly sparks joy for you. Go through photos, letters, and mementos, keeping only those that have a true personal significance.

Why "The Life-Changing Magic of Tidying Up" Stands Out:

Marie Kondo's "The Life-Changing Magic of Tidying Up" is not just a guide about decluttering; it's a philosophy of valuing the things that truly bring joy into one's life. Its unique and spiritual approach towards belongings encourages readers not just to tidy their physical space, but also to reflect on the kind of life they want to lead. The book resonates with many because it is not merely about cleaning; it's about resetting one's life and finding contentment in the everyday. The concept of expressing gratitude to belongings before parting with them also provides a fresh perspective that can lessen the emotional difficulty of letting go.

In including this title, we're acknowledging its profound influence on the world of decluttering and personal well-being. The book has not only transformed homes but also people's relationship with their possessions and the way they perceive joy and value in their everyday lives.

16

"12 Rules for Life: An Antidote to Chaos" by Jordan B. Peterson

12 Rules for Life: An Antidote to Chaos" by Jordan B. Peterson is a self-help book that provides life advice through essays on abstract ethical principles, psychology, mythology, religion, and personal anecdotes. Here's a thorough summary of the 12 rules presented in the book:

1. **Stand up straight with your shoulders back:** This rule uses the metaphor of lobsters to explain the importance of posture and dominance hierarchies. By standing tall, individuals can increase their serotonin levels, feel more confident, and are better prepared to confront life's challenges.

2. **Treat yourself like someone you are responsible for helping:** People often neglect their own needs. Peterson suggests that you should care for yourself with the same diligence you would use to care for another person.

3. **Make friends with people who want the best for you:** It's vital to surround yourself with positive, supportive

individuals. Avoid those who drag you down or foster negativity.

4. **Compare yourself to who you were yesterday, not to who someone else is today:** Each person's journey is unique, and comparing oneself to others can lead to envy and feelings of inadequacy. Instead, focus on personal growth and self-improvement.

5. **Do not let your children do anything that makes you dislike them:** As a parent, you should provide guidance and discipline. By setting boundaries, children can develop into responsible and ethical individuals.

6. **Set your house in perfect order before you criticize the world:** Before attempting to change or criticize the larger world, ensure that you've addressed your personal issues and have your life in order.

7. **Pursue what is meaningful (not what is expedient):** It's essential to seek long-term value and purpose rather than short-term gain. This rule delves into the biblical story of Cain and Abel, discussing resentment and the importance of sacrifice.

8. **Tell the truth — or, at least, don't lie:** Honesty establishes trust and lays the foundation for fruitful relationships and functional societies.

9. **Assume that the person you are listening to might know something you don't:** Genuine listening requires humility and the acknowledgment that others can provide valuable insights or knowledge.

10. **Be precise in your speech:** Clearly communicating your thoughts, needs, and boundaries can prevent unnecessary problems and misunderstandings.

11. **Do not bother children when they are skateboarding:**

Overprotection can stifle growth and resilience. This rule emphasizes the importance of allowing children (especially boys) to confront and overcome danger and challenges.

12. **Pet a cat when you encounter one on the street:** Life is fraught with challenges and suffering. However, it's essential to appreciate and find solace in small moments of beauty and happiness.

Why "12 Rules for Life" is Noteworthy:

Jordan B. Peterson's "12 Rules for Life" has generated significant attention and discussion, both positive and critical. The book intertwines psychological science, classical philosophy, religious stories, and personal anecdotes to provide guidance and perspective on leading a meaningful life. Whether one agrees or disagrees with all the premises presented, the book's depth and Peterson's erudition in various fields make it a significant contribution to the self-help genre. The book encourages readers to take responsibility for their lives, confront their personal dragons, and find meaning amidst the chaos.

17

"Breaking the Habit of Being Yourself" by Dr. Joe Dispenza

"Breaking the Habit of Being Yourself: How to Lose Your Mind and Create a New One" by Dr. Joe Dispenza delves into the intersection of neuroscience, quantum physics, and the power of positive thinking. The book offers a structured approach to break free from detrimental habits and self-imposed limits to achieve a more fulfilling, healthier, and conscious life.

Summary of Key Concepts and Themes:

1. **You Are Not Doomed by Your Genes:** Dispenza introduces the idea that people are not destined to a certain life because of their genetics. He challenges the deterministic view of genetics and instead promotes epigenetics – the concept that your environment and consciousness can influence the expression of your genes.

2. **Thoughts Can Change Reality:** Dispenza delves into

quantum physics to highlight how an observer can affect the nature of reality. He asserts that by changing our thoughts and emotions, we can change our personal realities.

3. **The Power of Meditation:** A major portion of the book is dedicated to meditation. Dispenza provides step-by-step guidance on how to meditate to break old patterns and create new habits. He believes that meditation can rewire the brain, allowing people to detach from old, unproductive habits and create new, beneficial ones.

4. **Overcoming the Past Self:** The book emphasizes the importance of shedding the past self and its limiting beliefs. Dispenza argues that memories from the past can keep people trapped in detrimental cycles, but by changing their internal states, they can break these cycles.

5. **Creating a New Mind for a New Future:** Dispenza encourages readers to envision and create their desired futures. By regularly and vividly imagining a better future, one can start manifesting that future in their current reality.

6. **The Role of Elevated Emotions:** Positive emotions such as love, joy, and gratitude can significantly impact the body at a cellular level. Cultivating these emotions can lead to better health, fulfillment, and well-being.

Practical Steps to Transformation:

Throughout the book, Dr. Dispenza provides a series of meditative exercises designed to help readers break the habit of being themselves and transform their lives. These exercises include:

- Overcoming past limitations and negative thought patterns.
- Formulating a clear intention of the future you want.
- Cultivating elevated emotions to help manifest that future.

Why "Breaking the Habit of Being Yourself" is Significant:

Dr. Joe Dispenza's "Breaking the Habit of Being Yourself" offers a blend of science, spirituality, and self-help. It demystifies complex concepts in neuroscience and quantum physics and presents them in a way that's accessible to the average reader. The book's underlying premise is empowering, suggesting that individuals have far more control over their lives and health than they might have believed. By providing practical tools and insights, Dispenza empowers readers to actively shape their futures, breaking free from past limitations.

18

"Daring to Lead" by Brené Brown

"Dare to Lead: Brave Work. Tough Conversations. Whole Hearts." is written by Brené Brown, a research professor known for her work on vulnerability, courage, empathy, and leadership. In "Dare to Lead," she focuses on how these themes play out in the world of leadership and organizational culture. Here's a detailed summary:

Overview

Brené Brown uses her extensive research to provide insights and tools necessary for effective, empathetic leadership. She argues that being a courageous leader means embracing vulnerability, which is not about winning or losing but about the courage to show up when you can't predict the outcome.

Key Concepts:

Rumbling with Vulnerability: Brown emphasizes that vulnerability is not a sign of weakness but a source of strength. Leaders should be open to feeling their emotions and expressing them. This is termed as "rumbling" with vulnerability, where leaders face tough situations with courage and clarity.

Living into Our Values: Leaders should not just identify their values but live them out in their behaviors. When actions align with values, it creates trust and integrity in leadership.

Braving Trust: Trust is the foundation of connection and leadership. Brown provides a mnemonic called "BRAVING" to breakdown the anatomy of trust:

- **B**oundaries
- **R**eliability
- **A**ccountability
- **V**ault (keeping confidences)
- **I**ntegrity
- **N**on-judgment
- **G**enerosity (assuming positive intent)

Learning to Rise: Leaders will inevitably face failures and setbacks. It's essential to learn from them and use them as a basis for growth. This requires resilience and the ability to "rise" from challenges.

Armored Leadership vs. Daring Leadership: Brown identifies common defensive tactics or "armors" leaders use to shield themselves from vulnerability (like perfectionism, cynicism, or power hoarding) and contrasts these with behaviors of daring leadership (like learning on the fly, making tough decisions, or owning up to mistakes).

Shame and Empathy: Shame is a powerful emotion in the workplace that can hinder growth, creativity, and innovation. Leaders should understand shame and cultivate empathy to counteract its effects.

Tools and Techniques: Throughout the book, Brown offers actionable strategies and tools, such as:

- **Clear is Kind:** Being clear in communication, expectations, and feedback is a kindness. Ambiguity or non-communication can lead to confusion, mistakes, and resentment.
- **The Square Squad:** Identify a small group of people whose opinions matter to you. Seeking constant approval from everyone is not only impractical but also counterproductive.
- **Paint Done:** When giving an assignment or discussing outcomes, be clear about what a successful completion looks like. This provides clarity and prevents wasted effort.

Why "Dare to Lead" is Noteworthy:

"Dare to Lead" by Brené Brown stands out because it takes a human-centric approach to leadership. Instead of relying on authority or power dynamics, Brown's model emphasizes connection, empathy, and vulnerability as sources of strength in leadership. By combining robust research with relatable anecdotes and actionable strategies, Brown offers a transformative roadmap for anyone in a leadership role or aspiring to step into one. The book encourages a shift from armored, defensive leadership styles to more open, courageous, and authentic approaches, which are essential in the ever-evolving, dynamic workplaces of today.

19

"The Obstacle Is the Way" by Ryan Holiday

"The Obstacle Is the Way: The Timeless Art of Turning Trials into Triumph" by Ryan Holiday draws inspiration from Stoicism, a school of Hellenistic philosophy, to provide guidance on turning obstacles into opportunities. Here's a detailed summary:

Overview

Ryan Holiday explores the idea that challenges and setbacks aren't to be feared or avoided. Instead, they can be harnessed as opportunities for growth, learning, and progress. Through a collection of historical anecdotes and biographical sketches, he underscores that many successful individuals and leaders throughout history have applied the principle of using obstacles as stepping stones to greatness.

Key Concepts:

1. **Perception:** How you perceive and interpret an event is more crucial than the event itself. A disciplined mind can turn obstacles into advantages. It's essential to see things dispassionately and objectively.
2. **Action:** Effective action is necessary to navigate through and overcome challenges. This requires persistence, flexibility, and an iterative approach. It's not about recklessly charging forward but about calculated and purposeful progression.
3. **Will:** This is the internal power and control you have, regardless of external events. While you can't always control what happens to you, you can control how you respond. This inner fortitude allows individuals to endure hardships and move forward.

Major Themes:

- **Embracing Resistance:** Similar to how muscles grow when met with resistance, individuals grow when they face challenges. Resistance, in many forms, helps refine and strengthen character.
- **Altering Perception:** Most obstacles are daunting because of how they are perceived. By changing one's perspective, what once seemed like a setback can become a path forward.
- **The Discipline of Action:** It's not enough to just think differently. Effective and consistent action, informed by a revised perception, is the key to navigating challenges.
- **The Power of Will:** While actions address external obstacles, willpower addresses internal barriers. Cultivating a

resilient will can help one endure and even thrive amidst adversity.

Noteworthy Historical Anecdotes:

Holiday draws from a myriad of stories from history to illustrate his points:

- **Thomas Edison:** When Edison's factory burned down, instead of being devastated, he remarked that the fire cleared out a lot of old inventory and set about rebuilding, turning a disaster into an opportunity for rejuvenation.
- **Amelia Earhart:** Before she became the first woman to fly across the Atlantic, she was given an opportunity to be a passenger on such a flight. Instead of seeing it as a slight, she took the opportunity, which eventually paved the way for her future solo flight.
- **Theodore Roosevelt:** Facing numerous health challenges in his early life, Roosevelt embraced a strenuous life, using his physical challenges as motivation to embrace action and adventure.

Why "The Obstacle Is the Way" is Significant:

Ryan Holiday's book serves as a manual for resilience, adapt-ability, and success in the face of challenges. Drawing upon the wisdom of Stoicism and myriad historical examples, it's a powerful reminder that we have the agency to transform obstacles into opportunities. It's not just a philosophy book but a practical guide to facing adversity in personal and professional life. The book resonates with readers because it offers a time-

tested approach to problems, emphasizing personal responsibility and the transformative power of perspective, action, and
will.

20

"Radical Acceptance" by Tara Brach

"Radical Acceptance: Embracing Your Life with the Heart of a Buddha" by Tara Brach is a book that combines insights from both Western psychology and Eastern spiritual practices, mainly Buddhism. Brach, a psychologist and meditation teacher, posits that feelings of unworthiness are a pervasive suffering in Western cultures. Through "Radical Acceptance," she offers a path to freedom from this pain. Here's an in-depth summary:

Overview

The core idea of "Radical Acceptance" is that our suffering primarily comes from our rejection of our present-moment experience, whether it's self-judgment, shame, or feelings of inadequacy. By fully accepting ourselves and our current situation, we can attain a more peaceful, fulfilled state of being.

Key Concepts:

1. **The Trance of Unworthiness:** Brach believes that many people live in a "trance of unworthiness," constantly feeling that they're not good enough. This is due to a combination of societal pressures, personal experiences, and internalized expectations.

2. **The Path of Radical Acceptance:** The remedy to this trance is the practice of radical acceptance, which involves fully embracing ourselves and our situation without judgment. This doesn't mean passive resignation but rather a deep, compassionate acknowledgment of reality.

3. **Mindfulness and Compassion:** These are the two wings of radical acceptance. Mindfulness allows us to see what's happening clearly, while compassion lets us hold what we see with kindness.

4. **The Sacred Pause:** One of the tools Brach introduces is the idea of taking a "sacred pause" — a moment to stop, breathe, and become present. This pause can be transformative, shifting us from a reaction mode to a response mode.

5. **Embracing Difficult Emotions:** Rather than running from difficult emotions like fear, anger, or grief, Brach suggests we should lean into them, exploring them with curiosity and compassion. By doing so, we can understand their roots and release their hold on us.

Major Themes:

- **Suffering and the False Refuge:** Many people try to escape pain through what Brach calls "false refuges" like addiction, overwork, or judgment. However, these only increase suffering. True refuge comes from facing our pain and extending compassion to ourselves.
- **The Power of Presence:** Being fully present, both with ourselves and others, is a powerful form of healing. When we're present, we can see reality clearly and respond from a place of wisdom and compassion.
- **Reconnecting with Our Bodily Experience:** Many people are disconnected from their bodies, especially when experiencing pain. Brach encourages readers to reconnect with their bodily sensations, as this can be a path to healing and understanding.
- **The Stories We Tell Ourselves:** A significant part of our suffering comes from the narratives we have about ourselves, others, and the world. By examining and, if necessary, rewriting these narratives, we can free ourselves from many self-imposed limitations.

Practical Techniques:

Throughout "Radical Acceptance," Brach provides various meditation exercises and techniques designed to cultivate mindfulness, compassion, and presence. These techniques guide readers through processes of self-inquiry, healing, and transformation.

Why "Radical Acceptance" is Noteworthy:

"Radical Acceptance" is significant because it addresses a deep-seated pain that many people feel but struggle to articulate — the sense of not being enough. Tara Brach offers a compassionate, insightful remedy to this pain, blending her understanding of psychology with profound spiritual insights. The book resonates with readers because it speaks to a universal human experience and offers tangible, tested tools for transformation. Whether one is familiar with Buddhism or not, Brach's teachings on acceptance, presence, and self-compassion are universally accessible and healing.

21

"The Road Less Traveled" by M. Scott Peck

"The Road Less Traveled: A New Psychology of Love, Traditional Values, and Spiritual Growth" by M. Scott Peck is a classic work that delves into the intricacies of life, love, and personal growth. Published in 1978, the book combines elements of psychology and spirituality to provide insights into the challenges of life and paths to personal development.

Overview

M. Scott Peck begins the book with the famous line, "Life is difficult." He argues that once we truly accept this fact, we can transcend it. Throughout the book, Peck explores the nature of love, the importance of discipline, and the stages of spiritual growth.

Key Concepts:

Accepting Responsibility: Peck emphasizes the importance of taking responsibility for our own actions, decisions, and lives. By doing so, we can solve problems effectively and grow spiritually.

Love is an Action: Peck provides a detailed exploration of love, arguing that true love is not a feeling but an activity and an investment. It involves extending oneself for the purpose of nurturing one's own or another's spiritual growth.

Discipline is Essential for Growth: Four tools of discipline, as described by Peck, are:

- **Delaying gratification:** The ability to put off something pleasurable now to gain something more valuable later.
- **Acceptance of responsibility:** Taking charge of one's own actions and decisions.
- **Dedication to truth:** Committing to reality at all costs.
- **Balancing:** The ability to navigate conflicting needs and demands.

Stages of Spiritual Growth: Peck outlines four stages of spiritual and psychological development:

- **Stage I – Chaotic/Antisocial:** Selfish, unprincipled, and ruled by the threat of punishment.
- **Stage II – Formal/Institutional:** Rule-bound and tied to established structures and beliefs. Most religious people are in this stage.

- **Stage III – Skeptic/Individual:** A stage of questioning the status quo and seeking one's own answers.
- **Stage IV – Mystic/Communal:** Finding a connection with others, recognizing the interconnectedness of things, and having a universal understanding.

Major Themes:

- **Growth and Religion:** The book delves deep into the nature of religion and spirituality, suggesting that true spiritual growth is about evolving and moving from one stage to the next, rather than sticking rigidly to dogmas.
- **The Nature of Evil:** Peck discusses the concept of evil, suggesting that it stems from a refusal to grow and an active resistance to the good.
- **Mental Health:** The book touches upon various aspects of mental health, arguing that many so-called "neuroses" and "psychological disorders" are better understood as reactions to life's inherent difficulties.

Why "The Road Less Traveled" is Significant:

M. Scott Peck's "The Road Less Traveled" is a landmark book because it bridges the gap between psychology and spirituality. Its holistic approach to personal growth resonates with many readers as it doesn't just treat the symptoms of life's challenges but delves deep into their causes. The book encourages readers to confront and embrace life's inherent difficulties, suggesting that this is the path to personal and spiritual evolution.

By combining profound psychological insights with equally profound spiritual wisdom, Peck provides a roadmap for genuine personal transformation. His emphasis on love, discipline, and growth offers a counter-narrative to the quick fixes of modern self-help culture, making "The Road Less Traveled" a timeless and essential read.

22

"So Good They Can't Ignore You" by Cal Newport

"So Good They Can't Ignore You: Why Skills Trump Passion in the Quest for Work You Love" by Cal Newport is a book that challenges the conventional advice of "follow your passion." Instead, Newport argues that passion comes after you become excellent at something valuable, not before. Here's an in-depth summary:

Overview

Cal Newport's primary message is that building rare and valuable skills (which he terms "career capital") is the key to finding fulfilling work. He argues against the idea of pre-existing passions determining the right job for individuals. Instead, Newport suggests that passion often comes after mastery.

Key Concepts:

The Passion Hypothesis: Newport identifies a widespread belief, the "Passion Hypothesis," which suggests that the key to a satisfying job is figuring out what you're passionate about and then finding a job aligned with that passion. He critiques this hypothesis, pointing out its flaws and the dissatisfaction it can lead to.

Craftsman Mindset vs. Passion Mindset: Newport introduces two mindsets:

- **Passion Mindset:** Focusing on what the world can offer you. This can lead to chronic unhappiness and self-centeredness in your career pursuits.
- **Craftsman Mindset:** Focusing on what you can offer the world. Adopting this mindset emphasizes the importance of becoming "so good they can't ignore you."

Acquiring Career Capital: Newport stresses the importance of acquiring "career capital" – these are the skills and expertise that make you valuable in any field. The best way to get this capital is through deliberate practice, pushing yourself out of your comfort zone, and constantly seeking feedback.

Control and Mission: Once you've acquired enough career capital, Newport says you can gain more control over your career, which in turn makes work more fulfilling. Eventually, this control can lead you to identify a "mission" or higher purpose in your work.

Major Themes:

- **The Limitation of Passion:** Newport consistently argues that passion is an unreliable guide in one's career. It's limited and often nebulous, leading people to jump from one job to another without ever finding satisfaction.

- **Value of Skills:** Newport suggests that in today's economy, what's rare and valuable are not pre-existing passions but hard-earned skills. By honing these skills, you increase your value and leverage in any field.

- **Deliberate Practice:** Newport emphasizes the importance of constantly pushing yourself in your job to gain more skills, even if it's uncomfortable. This principle of deliberate practice is borrowed from how experts train in various fields.

- **Finding a Mission:** Newport believes that after acquiring sufficient career capital and control, you'll be in a better position to identify a mission in your work, which can provide a deep sense of fulfillment and purpose.

Why "So Good They Can't Ignore You" is Significant:

Cal Newport's book stands out because it challenges the widespread "follow your passion" advice that's popular in many career-guidance circles. By pointing to real-world examples and weaving in evidence from various fields, Newport provides a compelling argument for a more skills-centric approach to career satisfaction.

For many readers, the book is an eye-opener, revealing that often, passion follows mastery and not the other way around. Newport's emphasis on deliberate practice, building career capital, and the craftsman mindset offers a refreshing and practical perspective on how to build a fulfilling career.

23

"Psycho-Cybernetics" by Maxwell Maltz

"Psycho-Cybernetics" by Dr. Maxwell Maltz is a seminal work in the self-help genre, published in 1960. Maltz, originally a plastic surgeon, realized that changing people's physical appearances sometimes didn't change their self-image or improve their happiness. This led him to explore the relationship between self-image and a person's ability to achieve (or fail to achieve) their goals. Here's a comprehensive summary:

Overview

At its core, "Psycho-Cybernetics" presents the idea that individuals possess a mental system, akin to a "success mechanism," that can be calibrated to achieve goals, much like a thermostat or a missile guidance system. This mechanism operates based on one's self-image, which, when adjusted or corrected, can lead to profound changes in a person's life.

Key Concepts:

1. **Self-Image:** Maltz posits that everyone has a mental picture of themselves, which dictates how they respond to the world. This self-image is built over years and is based on experiences, feedback, and interpretations of the world. If the self-image is flawed or negative, it can hold individuals back from achieving their goals.

2. **Automatic Success Mechanism:** The mind, according to Maltz, operates like a guidance system. When set towards a clear goal and when unimpeded by a negative self-image, this mechanism can guide individuals toward success in much the same way that a missile's guidance system directs it to a target.

3. **The Power of Visualization:** One of the ways to reprogram the self-image is through visualization. By repeatedly visualizing a positive outcome or a desired behavior, individuals can influence their subconscious mind and, by extension, their self-image.

4. **Relaxation and Trust:** Maltz emphasizes the importance of relaxation for the "success mechanism" to operate correctly. He suggests that trying too hard or becoming overly anxious can impede the mechanism. It's essential to trust in the subconscious mind's ability to achieve the goal.

5. **Dealing with Failure:** Everyone encounters failures or setbacks. Maltz encourages seeing these not as evidence of personal inadequacy but as feedback. Failures provide information and are opportunities for learning and course correction.

6. **Forgiveness:** Holding onto past grudges or lingering

78

negative emotions can impact one's self-image and hinder the success mechanism. Maltz stresses the importance of forgiving oneself and others to maintain a healthy self-image.

Major Themes:

- **Change from Within:** Maltz's experiences as a plastic surgeon demonstrated that external changes (like cosmetic surgery) don't always lead to internal happiness or confidence. True change and happiness come from adjusting one's self-image.
- **Role of the Subconscious:** Much of "Psycho-Cybernetics" revolves around the idea that the subconscious mind is a goal-striving mechanism. By feeding it positive, clear goals and images, individuals can achieve success.
- **Feedback System:** Maltz often compares the human mind to a missile guidance system. Just as a missile makes constant adjustments based on feedback to hit its target, humans too can adjust their actions based on feedback to achieve their goals.

Why "Psycho-Cybernetics" is Significant:

"Psycho-Cybernetics" is often considered a foundational work in the realm of self-help and personal development. Its concepts about self-image and the mind's automatic success mechanism have influenced many subsequent self-help authors and personal development trainers.

Maltz's work was revolutionary at the time, suggesting that

by changing one's self-image, individuals could dramatically alter the course of their lives. His combination of psychological insights with practical advice offers readers a roadmap for achieving their goals and leading a more fulfilling life.

24

"Good to Great" by Jim Collins

"Good to Great: Why Some Companies Make the Leap... and Others Don't" is a well-regarded management book by Jim Collins, published in 2001. The book is a result of a comprehensive study carried out by Collins and his research team, where they analyzed companies that made the transition from good to outstanding performance and sustained it for at least fifteen years. Here's a detailed summary:

Overview

Collins and his team identified a set of elite companies that made the leap to great results and sustained those results for at least fifteen years. The research focused on understanding what distinguished these "great" companies from their comparison set, companies that either never made the leap or whose success was fleeting.

Key Concepts:

Level 5 Leadership: The top-performing companies were led by what Collins termed "Level 5" leaders. These leaders blend personal humility with professional will. They are self-effacing, modest, and more interested in the success of the company than personal accolades.

First Who, Then What: Before determining the direction of the company, the good-to-great companies focused on getting the right people onboard (and the wrong people off) and then figuring out the best path forward.

The Hedgehog Concept: The best companies understood their core business deeply and stuck to it. This idea is based on the parable of the fox, who knows many things, and the hedgehog, who knows one big thing. Great companies focused on where these three circles intersect:

- What they can be best in the world at
- What they are deeply passionate about
- What drives their economic engine

Culture of Discipline: Successful companies maintain a culture where disciplined people take disciplined action, aligned with the Hedgehog Concept, without bureaucracy or excessive controls.

The Flywheel and the Doom Loop: Greatness is not a function of circumstance but is a matter of conscious choice and discipline. Success is cumulative, not revolutionary. This concept imagines a massive flywheel that builds momentum turn by turn, move by move, culminating in breakthrough momentum. In contrast, companies that jump from one new initiative or strategy to another find themselves in a "doom loop," which is counterproductive.

Technology Accelerators: Good-to-great companies use technology to accelerate their momentum, not create it. They adopt new technologies if and only if they align with their Hedgehog Concept.

The Stockdale Paradox: Named after Admiral Jim Stockdale, this principle is about confronting the brutal facts of one's current reality while retaining faith that they will prevail in the end, regardless of the difficulties.

Major Themes:

- **Sustained Excellence:** The research focuses on companies that didn't just achieve temporary greatness but maintained it over a long period.
- **Simplicity and Clarity:** The best companies had a clear understanding of their strengths and strategy and didn't spread themselves too thin.
- **People Before Strategy:** Ensuring the company has the right team is more crucial than any single strategic decision.

Why "Good to Great" is Significant:

"Good to Great" became a defining management study because it was rooted in rigorous research rather than anecdotal observations. Collins and his team systematically identified and studied companies that had made the transition to greatness, and the book's findings have had a significant impact on how businesses think about leadership, strategy, and success.

The book's emphasis on humble leadership, clear focus, discipline, and the role of people in an organization's success offers a counter-narrative to flashy leadership and short-term strategies. "Good to Great" provides a roadmap for companies aiming for sustained, long-term excellence.

25

"Crucial Conversations" by Kerry Patterson, Joseph Grenny, Ron McMillan, and Al SwitzlerChatGPT

"Crucial Conversations: Tools for Talking When Stakes Are High" by Kerry Patterson, Joseph Grenny, Ron McMillan, and Al Switzler is a guide for handling difficult and important conversations. The book provides insights and tools for discussing tough topics at work and in personal life, and it emphasizes the importance of open dialogue for effective decision-making and improved relationships.

Overview

A "crucial conversation" is defined as a discussion between two or more people where stakes are high, opinions vary, and emotions run strong. The authors argue that effectively navigating such conversations can lead to better outcomes in almost all areas of life.

Key Concepts:

1. **Start with Heart:** Examine your motives for entering the conversation and decide what you truly want from it. This introspection ensures you approach the conversation with clarity and genuine intent.
2. **Learn to Look:** Be aware of the signs that a conversation is becoming crucial. Notice your own behavior, look for signs of safety or danger in others, and pay attention to the flow of dialogue.
3. **Make It Safe:** People don't engage in meaningful dialogue if they don't feel safe. When individuals feel threatened, they either become silent (withdrawing from the conversation) or violent (dominating the conversation). Ensure safety by establishing mutual respect and mutual purpose.
4. **Master My Stories:** How we act is based on the stories we tell ourselves. By reinterpreting our stories, we can control our emotions and handle crucial conversations better.
5. **State My Path:** Express your views in a way that is both honest and respectful. Avoid accusations, and instead, explain your perspective using facts and your feelings.
6. **Explore Others' Paths:** Encourage others to share their perspectives. Listen actively and ask questions to understand their viewpoint fully.
7. **Move to Action:** Conclude your conversation by ensuring clear action items, decisions, and expectations. Decide who does what by when.

Major Themes:

- **Open Dialogue:** The essence of the book is promoting open dialogue. When people can openly discuss high-stakes topics, relationships improve, and better decisions are made.
- **Safety:** For meaningful conversations to occur, all participants must feel safe enough to express their true feelings and beliefs.
- **Self-awareness:** A lot of the book's strategies focus on introspection—understanding one's feelings, examining one's motives, and being aware of one's behavior during a conversation.
- **Mutual Respect and Mutual Purpose:** Establishing common ground and showing respect, even in disagreements, is key to productive dialogue.

Why "Crucial Conversations" is Significant:

"Crucial Conversations" stands out for its actionable insights into a common challenge everyone faces: how to communicate effectively when emotions run high and there's a lot at stake. The book's guidelines have been widely adopted in corporate training programs, interpersonal relationship guidance, and conflict resolution scenarios.

The authors, through their extensive research and vast experience, provide a blueprint for how to handle conversations that matter the most. The tools and strategies they share not only aim to produce better results from these discussions but also to foster stronger relationships and create more effective teams and communities.

26

"Eat That Frog!" by Brian Tracy

"Eat That Frog!" by Brian Tracy is a book about time management and productivity. The title refers to a metaphor about tackling the most challenging tasks of one's day. The central premise is that if you start your day by "eating a frog" (doing the most significant and least appealing task first), then the rest of the day will be smoother by comparison. Here's a detailed summary:

Overview:

The book is organized into 21 chapters, each offering a specific technique or principle for improving productivity and time management. Tracy's advice is grounded in the idea that effective time management is crucial for success, and by focusing on important tasks and resisting the urge to procrastinate, individuals can achieve more in less time.

Key Concepts:

1. **"Eat That Frog!"**: Start your day by tackling the most significant, most important, and often the most challenging task first. Once you've completed this task, you'll gain momentum and a sense of accomplishment that will carry through the rest of the day.

2. **Determine Your Goals**: Clearly define your goals and write them down. Knowing what you want to achieve helps you prioritize your tasks and focus your energy on what truly matters.

3. **80/20 Rule**: Based on the Pareto Principle, 20% of your activities will account for 80% of your results. Thus, you should focus on those high-impact tasks that lead to the most significant results.

4. **ABCDE Method**: Label your tasks from A to E based on their importance. 'A' tasks are the most crucial, while 'E' tasks are the least important. Always focus on your 'A' tasks first.

5. **Key Result Areas**: Identify and focus on tasks that lead to results in your job or business. Know what you are expected to deliver and make sure you prioritize those tasks.

6. **Obstacle Analysis**: Determine what is holding you back from achieving your goals. Often, addressing a significant obstacle can have a profound effect on your productivity.

7. **Law of Forced Efficiency**: This law states that "There is never enough time to do everything, but there is always enough time to do the most important thing." It's about being clear on priorities.

8. **Prepare in Advance**: Begin with planning. Before start-

ing your day, list the tasks you need to accomplish and organize them based on priority.

9. **Batch Tasks and Time Blocking**: Group similar tasks together and handle them in a single time block, minimizing the start-up and slow-down times.

10. **Upgrade Your Skills**: Invest time in learning and improving the skills necessary for your key tasks.

Major Themes:

- **Procrastination**: One of the primary obstacles to productivity is the habit of delaying important tasks. Tracy offers multiple strategies to overcome procrastination.
- **Prioritization**: Not all tasks are created equal. Focusing on high-value tasks leads to better results.
- **Clarity and Focus**: Having clear goals and a sense of purpose allows for more focused and efficient work.

Why "Eat That Frog!" is Significant:

"Eat That Frog!" has become a staple in the realm of productivity literature due to its straightforward, actionable advice. Tracy doesn't just provide theories; he gives readers a step-by-step guide to being more effective in their work and personal lives.

The idea of tackling the most challenging task first—of "eating the frog"—is a simple yet powerful concept that resonates with many people. By addressing the most daunting tasks head-on, individuals can reduce stress, increase their productivity, and gain a sense of accomplishment that fuels further achievement.

27

"Switch" by Dan Heath and Chip Heath

"Switch: How to Change Things When Change Is Hard" is a book by brothers Chip and Dan Heath. It provides insights into the psychology of change and offers a framework for driving successful change in one's personal life, business, or society. The Heaths present the central metaphor of a Rider (the rational side), an Elephant (the emotional side), and the Path (the surrounding environment) to illustrate the complexities of effecting change.

Overview:

"Switch" delves into why it's often so tough to make lasting changes in both our personal and professional lives and offers a comprehensive set of solutions, rooted in psychological and organizational studies.

Key Concepts:

1. **The Rider (Rational Side):** This represents our logical and analytical side. The Rider loves to think long-term, ponder over endless information, and analyze matters. But it can easily get paralyzed by analysis, leading to inaction.
2. **The Elephant (Emotional Side):** The Elephant is driven by emotion and seeks immediate gratification. It is powerful, filled with love, sympathy, and loyalty, but can also be easily swayed by short-term rewards or personal desires. If the Rider and Elephant disagree on where to go, the Elephant usually wins due to its sheer power.
3. **The Path (Environment):** This is the surrounding environment that can shape the journey of the Rider and the Elephant. By tweaking the Path, change can become much easier, as both the Rider and the Elephant prefer to travel on a clear, easy route.

Strategies for Change:

Direct the Rider:

- **Find the Bright Spots:** Instead of focusing on problems, investigate what's working and clone it.
- **Script the Critical Moves:** Avoid analysis paralysis by providing clear instructions.
- **Point to the Destination:** Change becomes easier when you know where you're heading and why it's worth it.

Motivate the Elephant:

- **Find the Feeling:** Knowing something isn't enough to cause change; make people feel something.
- **Shrink the Change:** Break down the change so it doesn't feel too big and daunting.
- **Grow Your People:** Cultivate a sense of identity and instill a growth mindset.

Shape the Path:

- **Tweak the Environment:** When the situation changes, the behavior changes. Make changes in the environment to foster the desired behavior.
- **Build Habits:** When behavior becomes a habit, it's automatic and doesn't tax the Rider.
- **Rally the Herd:** Behavior is contagious; help spread it.

Major Themes:

- **System vs. Individuals:** Often, problems are due to the system and not the people. Altering the environment can significantly affect behavior.
- **Clarity of Direction:** One reason change initiatives fail is that the direction isn't clear. Providing a clear path can be the key to success.
- **Emotional Motivation:** The emotional side is vital for driving change. People need to feel the change on a visceral level.

Why "Switch" is Significant:

"Switch" stands out because it offers a comprehensive framework that accounts for both the rational and emotional aspects of change. The Heaths' approach is both systematic and empathetic, emphasizing that successful change requires aligning one's rational side, emotional side, and the environment.

Their model has been influential in various fields, from business management to social work, because it's versatile and holistic. The real-world examples they use to illustrate their points span different sectors and scales, making the book's concepts widely relatable and applicable.

28

"Quiet: The Power of Introverts in a World That Can't Stop Talking" by Susan Cain

"Quiet: The Power of Introverts in a World That Can't Stop Talking" by Susan Cain offers a deep dive into the world of introverts, challenging the modern-day Western culture's extrovert ideal. Cain provides a comprehensive look at the strengths and capabilities of introverts, how they are undervalued, and how they can shine in a society that often celebrates extroversion.

Overview:

"Quiet" asserts that the cultural bias towards extroversion in the West overlooks the valuable contributions of introverts. Susan Cain argues that introverts bring extraordinary talents and abilities to the world and should be encouraged and celebrated.

Key Concepts:

1. **The Extrovert Ideal:** Western culture, particularly in America, celebrates the "alpha" personality: gregarious, alpha, risk-taking. This extrovert ideal permeates our schools, workplaces, and institutions, often sidelining introverts.

2. **Introvert vs. Extrovert:** Introverts are people who thrive in more low-key environments and often feel more alive and energized in solitary or in one-on-one interactions. Extroverts, on the other hand, crave large amounts of stimulation and thrive in busier environments.

3. **The Neurology of Introversion:** Introversion and extroversion are rooted in neurobiology. Research indicates differences in how introverts and extroverts process stimuli and how their brains react to dopamine.

4. **The Power of Introverts:** While society often emphasizes quick decisions and group work, introverts shine in deeper thinking, persistence, and working independently. They're often more reflective and can produce high-quality work when allowed to focus deeply.

5. **The Cost of Denying True Nature:** Pushing introverts to fit into an extroverted mold can lead to physical and emotional health problems. Moreover, society misses out on the potential contributions from those who feel pressured to conform.

6. **Rethinking Groupthink:** The modern emphasis on group work and brainstorming can stifle creativity. Introverts often work best when they have time to think deeply and independently about problems.

7. **How to Love, Work with, and Raise an Introvert:** Intro-

verts have unique needs and strengths. Recognizing these can lead to more fulfilling relationships and more effective collaboration in the workplace.

Major Themes:

- **Value of Solitude:** One of the critical strengths of introverts is their ability to work alone. Solitude can foster creativity and deep thinking.
- **Cultural Differences:** Not all cultures value extroversion to the same degree. For instance, many Eastern cultures respect introspection and caution.
- **Nature vs. Nurture:** While there are biological bases for introversion and extroversion, culture and upbringing play a significant role in shaping behavior.
- **Embracing Introversion:** Rather than seeing introversion as something to overcome, it should be embraced for the unique strengths and perspectives it offers.

Why "Quiet" is Significant:

"Quiet" has resonated deeply with readers, particularly introverts, who often felt undervalued in a world that celebrates extroverted traits. Susan Cain's rigorous research, combined with personal anecdotes and real-world examples, provides a compelling argument for the reevaluation of introverted strengths.

The book has sparked conversations about the value of quiet, thoughtful individuals in schools, workplaces, and other institutions. It's been influential in promoting a more inclusive understanding of personality and temperament, recognizing that everyone, whether introverted or extroverted, has unique strengths to offer.

29

"The One Thing" by Gary Keller and Jay Papasan

"The One Thing: The Surprisingly Simple Truth Behind Extraordinary Results" by Gary Keller and Jay Papasan presents a focused approach to work and life by advocating that concentration on a single, most important task can lead to increased productivity and success.

Overview:

The central premise of "The One Thing" is that by concentrating your energy and effort on the single most important task in any given domain of your life, you can achieve extraordinary results. Spreading oneself thin across multiple tasks or goals can dilute the impact, while zeroing in on the most critical task allows for breakthroughs and significant accomplishments.

Key Concepts:

1. **The Domino Effect:** Much like how a line of dominoes falls with a push to just one, focusing on the most significant task will set off a chain of events that will lead to the desired result. Small, sequential actions can culminate in considerable outcomes.

2. **Success is Sequential, Not Simultaneous:** You can't do everything at the same time and achieve success. By focusing on one thing at a time, you can achieve sequential successes.

3. **The Focusing Question:** "What's the ONE Thing I can do such that by doing it everything else will be easier or unnecessary?" This question can help you identify your most crucial task at any given moment.

4. **Avoiding Multitasking:** Contrary to popular belief, multitasking is not effective. It dilutes focus and reduces productivity.

5. **The Lies that Mislead and Derail Us:** These include the belief in everything mattering equally, multitasking, a disciplined life, willpower always being on will-call, and a balanced life. The book posits that these are misconceptions that prevent us from focusing on our ONE Thing.

6. **The Four Thieves of Productivity:** These are the inability to say "no," the fear of chaos, poor health habits, and an environment that doesn't support your goals.

Major Themes:

- **Focus on Priority:** The book emphasizes the importance of prioritizing tasks, suggesting that not everything on your to-do list is equally important.
- **Work-Life Balance:** Keller and Papasan argue that balance isn't about giving equal attention to all areas of life but rather giving intense focus in one's most important areas at appropriate times.
- **The Power of Habits:** Building habits around your ONE Thing can lead to consistent and long-term results.
- **Time Blocking:** The authors advocate for setting aside large chunks of uninterrupted time (time blocks) dedicated to your most important tasks.

Why "The One Thing" is Significant:

"The One Thing" has resonated with many readers and professionals because of its straightforward approach to productivity. In an age of constant distractions and overwhelming to-do lists, the book's emphasis on simplicity and focus provides a refreshing perspective.

Keller and Papasan's insights challenge the common beliefs about multitasking and work-life balance, offering a new framework to approach both personal and professional goals. By concentrating on the most impactful tasks and activities, individuals can achieve more with less effort.

30

"The Book of Joy" by Dalai Lama and Desmond Tutu

"The Book of Joy: Lasting Happiness in a Changing World" is a heartwarming exploration of joy, happiness, and the meaning of life. The book is the product of a week-long conversation between two of the world's most respected spiritual leaders, the Dalai Lama and Archbishop Desmond Tutu, facilitated by co-author Douglas Abrams. Their dialogue, which took place in Dharamsala, India, to celebrate the Dalai Lama's 80th birthday, delves into the challenges of living a joyful life amidst inevitable sufferings and offers profound insights on how to achieve lasting happiness.

Overview:

Despite being exiled from his home country and facing many adversities throughout his life, the Dalai Lama radiates happiness and peace. Similarly, Desmond Tutu, despite confronting the immense challenges of apartheid in South Africa, remains an emblem of joy. In their conversations, they explore how they maintain joy amidst hardship and how others can achieve a similar state of mind and spirit.

Key Concepts:

1. **Nature of True Joy:** Both leaders assert that true joy is deeper and more enduring than happiness. While happiness is often dependent on external circumstances, joy arises from inner contentment and compassion.
2. **Pillars of Joy:** The Dalai Lama and Archbishop Tutu identify eight pillars of joy, which they categorize as either qualities of the mind or qualities of the heart:
3. *Mind Qualities:* Perspective, Humility, Humor, and Acceptance.
4. *Heart Qualities:* Forgiveness, Gratitude, Compassion, and Generosity.
5. **Dealing with Suffering:** Both spiritual leaders agree that suffering is an inevitable part of the human experience. However, one's perspective on suffering can influence its impact. By embracing suffering as a way to deepen compassion and understanding, individuals can find deeper meaning and joy in life.
6. **Power of Perspective:** How one perceives events determines their emotional response. By shifting perspectives, it's possible to reframe challenges as opportunities for growth.
7. **Importance of Human Connection:** Both leaders emphasize the significance of human connection and compassion. Interacting with others with a genuine sense of concern and compassion can be a profound source of joy.

Major Themes:

- **Interconnectedness:** Both the Dalai Lama and Desmond Tutu believe in the interconnectedness of all beings. This shared humanity is the foundation for compassion and understanding.
- **Transcendence of Religion:** While both leaders come from different religious backgrounds (Buddhism and Christianity, respectively), they find common ground in their beliefs about compassion, kindness, and the nature of joy. Their dialogue underscores the idea that joy and compassion transcend religious boundaries.
- **Overcoming Adversity:** Both leaders have faced immense personal and societal challenges. Their stories and insights underscore the idea that joy is attainable even amidst adversity.

Why "The Book of Joy" is Significant:

"The Book of Joy" provides readers with a unique opportunity to gain insights from two of the world's most revered spiritual figures. Their combined wisdom, presented through warm-hearted conversations, offers guidance on living a joyful life in the face of challenges. Their message of hope, resilience, and the enduring power of compassion resonates deeply with readers around the world, making it a significant contribution to contemporary spiritual literature.

31

"Deep Work" by Cal Newport

"Deep Work: Rules for Focused Success in a Distracted World" is a book by Cal Newport that delves into the benefits of deep, focused work and provides strategies to achieve it. Newport, a computer science professor at Georgetown University, argues that the ability to focus without distraction on a cognitively demanding task, which he calls "deep work," is increasingly rare in our age of constant digital distractions, but it's also more valuable than ever.

Overview:

"Deep Work" is divided into two main parts. The first part makes the case for the value and importance of deep work in today's fast-paced, digital world, while the second part offers practical advice and rules on how to cultivate deep work in one's own life.

Key Concepts:

1. **Definition of Deep Work:** Newport defines deep work as the ability to focus without distraction on a cognitively demanding task. It's a state of flow where one can produce the best work in less time.

2. **Value of Deep Work:** In the knowledge economy, those who can perform deep work are more likely to excel and advance in their careers. Deep work leads to mastery, innovation, and high-quality output.

3. **Shallow Work vs. Deep Work:** Newport contrasts deep work with shallow work, tasks that are non-cognitively demanding and often executed while distracted. Examples include routine emails and attending unnecessary meetings. While these tasks might be unavoidable, they should be minimized to prioritize deep work.

4. **Cultural Barriers to Deep Work:** Our culture, with its emphasis on instant communication and the rise of social media, has created an environment where distractions are the norm. Newport argues that this culture undervalues deep work, making it all the more important for individuals to recognize its value.

Major Themes:

- **Digital Minimalism:** Newport advocates for a conscious and minimal use of digital tools. Not all technology or platforms add value to one's life, and it's crucial to choose tools that serve one's goals and reject those that detract from them.

- **Routines and Rituals:** One of the ways to cultivate deep work is to establish routines and rituals that minimize the willpower required to transition into a state of deep focus.

· **Rest and Downtime:** Newport emphasizes that downtime aids insights, replenishes energy, and is essential for a productive deep work schedule.

Rules and Strategies:

1. **Work Deeply:** Newport suggests different philosophies or schedules to integrate deep work into one's routine, such as the monastic philosophy (eliminating or radically minimizing shallow obligations) and the rhythmic philosophy (setting aside specific times each day for deep work).

2. **Embrace Boredom:** Train yourself to resist distractions. Don't automatically turn to your phone or computer when you're bored; this trains your mind to seek and expect constant stimulation.

3. **Quit Social Media:** Newport doesn't suggest everyone should quit social media but recommends evaluating if these platforms are the best use of one's time.

4. **Drain the Shallows:** Minimize shallow work by being conscious of how much time these tasks consume and by scheduling them tightly.

Why "Deep Work" is Significant:

In an era where distractions are omnipresent, and attention is fragmented, "Deep Work" provides a timely and essential guide on harnessing the power of focused concentration. Newport's argument is backed by numerous examples from various fields, showing that deep work is crucial for anyone wishing to achieve excellence, innovation, and meaningful results. The book serves as a counter-narrative to the prevailing culture of constant connectivity and offers actionable strategies for those seeking more profound satisfaction and success in their professional lives.

32

"As a Man Thinketh" by James Allen

"As a Man Thinketh" is a self-help classic written by James Allen, published in 1903. It is a short book, but its powerful message has made it a seminal work in the personal development field. The book's central thesis is that one's thoughts shape one's reality; thus, by controlling and directing one's thoughts, one can control and direct one's destiny.

Overview:

Drawing inspiration from a verse in the Book of Proverbs ("As a man thinketh in his heart, so is he"), Allen's work delves into the profound influence of thoughts on character, circumstances, health, purpose, and achievements. He believes that the mind is like a garden that, if cultivated, can produce flowers of joy, but if neglected, can produce weeds of suffering.

Key Concepts:

1. **Thought and Character:** Allen states that a person's character is the complete sum of their thoughts. Just as plants cannot grow without seeds, actions cannot occur without preceding thoughts.

2. **Effect of Thought on Circumstances:** Rather than circumstances shaping a man, it is a man who shapes his circumstances with his thoughts. By nurturing positive thoughts, one can overcome adverse circumstances.

3. **Thought and Purpose:** Allen asserts that until thought is linked with purpose, there is no intelligent accomplishment. With the absence of purpose, one becomes susceptible to petty worries, fears, and self-pity.

4. **The Thought-Factor in Achievement:** Contrary to the belief that external factors determine success, Allen believes that strength of purpose, enthusiasm, and focused effort, all products of the mind, are the true determinants.

5. **Visions and Ideals:** The dreamers are the saviors of the world. By dreaming, one sets the blueprint, and through continuous and purposeful thought, one can realize those dreams.

6. **Serenity:** Achieving a calm state of mind, regardless of external conditions, is the result of long and patient effort in self-control. Serenity is the crown of self-controlled, deliberate thought.

Major Themes:

- **Responsibility:** Allen emphasizes personal responsibility, suggesting that individuals have the power to change their lives by changing their thoughts.
- **Mind as a Garden:** One of the book's enduring metaphors is that of a garden. Just as a gardener cultivates his garden, removing weeds and planting flowers, individuals must tend to the garden of their mind, weeding out negative thoughts and cultivating positive ones.
- **The Power of Thought:** The cornerstone of Allen's philosophy is the transformative power of thought. Positive thoughts lead to positive outcomes, while negative thoughts lead to adversity.
- **Inner World Shapes the Outer World:** Allen suggests that external circumstances reflect internal thoughts. By changing one's inner world of thoughts, one can change the outer world of circumstances.

Why "As a Man Thinketh" is Significant:

"As a Man Thinketh" has endured as a cornerstone of self-help literature for over a century. Its message, emphasizing the power of individual thought in shaping life's outcomes, has resonated with countless readers and influenced many contemporary self-help authors. Allen's work promotes personal empowerment, responsibility, and the idea that we are the architects of our own destiny. Its concise yet profound insights make it a must-read for those on a personal development journey.

33

"The Miracle Morning" by Hal Elrod

"The Miracle Morning: The Not-So-Obvious Secret Guaranteed to Transform Your Life (Before 8AM)" is a self-help book by Hal Elrod. In it, Elrod presents a morning routine designed to help individuals maximize their potential and achieve their goals. The routine, which he calls the "Life S.A.V.E.R.S.," is based on six practices that have been hailed for their positive impact on personal and professional success.

Overview:

Hal Elrod's "The Miracle Morning" is predicated on the belief that how you start your day largely determines the quality of your day, your work, and your life. By dedicating time each morning to personal development and growth, individuals can create a purposeful and productive morning routine that sets a positive tone for the rest of the day.

The Life S.A.V.E.R.S: The core of Elrod's morning routine is the

Life S.A.V.E.R.S., an acronym representing six practices:

1. **S – Silence:** This can be achieved through meditation, prayer, reflection, or deep breathing. The purpose is to calm the mind, reduce stress, and cultivate a state of peace.
2. **A – Affirmations:** Positive statements that reinforce your goals and the person you want to become. They are designed to reprogram your thinking, boost self-confidence, and reinforce a positive mindset.
3. **V – Visualization:** By imagining the completion of your goals and the steps needed to achieve them, you can increase motivation and clarify the actions needed.
4. **E – Exercise:** A morning workout can help boost energy, enhance health, and improve mood. Even a short, consistent workout can yield significant benefits.
5. **R – Reading:** Investing in personal growth by reading books or materials that educate, inspire, and provide knowledge.
6. **S – Scribing:** Journaling about gratitude, lessons learned, and affirmations. This helps in processing thoughts, tracking personal growth, and maintaining focus on what's important.

Key Takeaways:

- **Morning Routine is Crucial:** Elrod believes that a dedicated morning routine is foundational for success and well-being. By starting the day with intention and purpose, you can set a positive trajectory for the rest of the day.
- **Consistency Over Duration:** It's not about the amount of time you dedicate to the Life S.A.V.E.R.S. but the consistency

with which you do them. Even a short duration spent genuinely can be transformative.

- **Overcoming Challenges:** Elrod emphasizes that challenges and setbacks, including his personal experiences of being clinically dead for six minutes after a car accident and later facing financial ruin, can be overcome with the right mindset and habits.

Why "The Miracle Morning" is Significant:

Hal Elrod's "The Miracle Morning" has resonated with readers worldwide due to its actionable advice and its potential to instigate real change in one's life. By highlighting the importance of mornings as a launchpad for a successful day and life, Elrod provides a framework that individuals can adapt to their own needs. The idea is not to add more tasks to an already busy day but to optimize the morning hours as a time of personal growth and self-improvement. The book's emphasis on personal accountability and proactive living has made it a favorite among entrepreneurs, professionals, and individuals looking to improve their overall quality of life.

34

"Solve for Happy" by Mo Gawdat

In "Solve for Happy," Mo Gawdat, a former Chief Business Officer for Google [X], takes a scientific and systematic approach to happiness. Drawing from his engineering background, he presents a model aiming to make the happiness equation more predictable and attainable.

The Happiness Equation:

- Gawdat introduces a straightforward premise: **Happiness ≥ Your perception of the events in your life – Your expectations of how life should behave.**
- In essence, it's not the actual events in our lives that dictate our happiness, but how we perceive these events in relation to our expectations.

Illusions:

- Gawdat identifies a series of "illusions" that cloud our understanding of reality, leading to unhappiness. These include our perceptions of thought, self, knowledge, time, and control.

- By recognizing and understanding these illusions, we can recalibrate our perceptions to align more closely with reality.

Blind Spots:

- Just as illusions distort our perceptions, Gawdat argues that there are "blind spots" in our thinking which can skew our understanding of events. Recognizing these cognitive biases can help rectify our distortions.

Seven Ultimate Truths:

- Gawdat lists out truths that, when accepted, can lead to a more consistent state of happiness. These include the reality of now (living in the present), the impermanence of life, and the idea that change is the only constant.

Personal Tragedy and Perspective:

- Gawdat's motivation for the book and his exploration of happiness stems from personal tragedy. The unexpected death of his son spurred him on a journey to understand the nature of happiness and how it can be sustained even amidst profound pain.
- His perspective is both introspective and universally applicable, emphasizing that while pain is inevitable, suffering is optional.

6-7-5 Framework:

- **6** illusions that cloud our worldview.
- **7** blind spots that distort our perception of events.
- **5** ultimate truths that, when accepted, can lead to lasting happiness.

Why "Solve for Happy" Offers a Unique Perspective on Happiness:

Mo Gawdat's approach to happiness stands out for its fusion of logic, engineering principles, and personal introspection. His analytical method to deconstructing happiness aims to make the emotion more attainable and less elusive. For those who appreciate structured, logical approaches to life's intangibles, "Solve for Happy" provides a refreshing and insightful perspective. Furthermore, Gawdat's personal journey and vulnerability in sharing his own experiences lend the book a profound authenticity.

35

"The Power of Habit" by Charles Duhigg

"The Power of Habit" delves into the science of why habits exist and how they can be transformed. Drawing from academic studies, interviews, and real-life examples, Duhigg explores the neurological and psychological mechanisms behind our habits and offers practical insights into changing them.

1. The Anatomy of Habits

At the core of Duhigg's exploration is the "habit loop," a three-part process that governs the formation and function of habits:

- **Cue:** A trigger that tells the brain to go into automatic mode and which habit to use.
- **Routine:** The behavior itself, which can be emotional, physical, or mental.
- **Reward:** A positive stimulus that reinforces the habit loop.

Over time, the brain begins to associate the cue with the reward, making the routine more automatic. This cycle can be applied to individual habits (like smoking or snacking) or organizational habits (like the routines businesses follow).

2. The Golden Rule of Habit Change

Duhigg outlines the "Golden Rule of Habit Change," which is that the most successful habit changes involve identifying and maintaining the old cue and reward, but swapping out the routine. This process requires belief, often facilitated by community or group support.

3. Keystone Habits

Keystone habits are powerful because they create a domino effect in other areas of one's life or an organization. By focusing on changing or cultivating one significant habit, it can lead to a series of changes across various aspects of life. An example is exercise, which can lead to better eating habits, improved productivity, and a more structured routine.

4. Habits in Business and Organizations

Businesses and organizations have habits too. For companies to change, leaders need to recognize the patterns that exist and work to shift them. Duhigg cites several case studies, such as Alcoa's focus on safety habits under CEO Paul O'Neill, leading to significant positive changes across the organization.

5. The Power of Crisis

Crises can serve as the perfect opportunity for organizations to reshape habits. When routines are disrupted, it's an opportune time to instigate new patterns of behavior.

6. The Freedom of Habit

The book closes by examining the balance between habits (which can be constraining) and the freedom that comes when one gains mastery over them. By understanding and altering habits, people can reclaim control over their behaviors and ultimately, their lives.

Why "The Power of Habit" is Significant:

"The Power of Habit" is a pivotal work because it demystifies an integral aspect of human behavior: our habits. By combining narratives, case studies, and scientific research, Duhigg offers readers not just an understanding of how habits work but also actionable steps to harness and change them. In an era where self-improvement and efficiency are highly sought after, this book provides tools and insights that can profoundly impact individual lives and organizational structures. It's a testament to the potential for transformation when we understand the mechanisms driving our actions.

36

"The Subtle Art of Not Giving a F*ck" by Mark Manson

Mark Manson's "The Subtle Art of Not Giving a F*ck" offers a counterintuitive approach to living a good life. Instead of promoting relentless positivity and endless pursuits of happiness, Manson advises readers to embrace life's limitations, confront its painful truths, and accept its uncertainties. The book serves as an antidote to the conventional self-help genre, focusing on values, acceptance, and the understanding that life is inherently imperfect.

1. The "Not Giving a F*ck" Paradox
At the outset, Manson explains the book's title is not about indifference but about being comfortable with being different. The core idea is to give a f*ck about only what is true and immediate and important.

2. The Feedback Loop from Hell
Modern society has an obsession with unending positivity, but Manson suggests that this can become a feedback loop. The

more we aim for positivity, the more we recognize what we lack, creating a cycle of negativity.

3. You Are Not Special

Contrary to the prevailing narrative that everyone is exceptional, Manson asserts that most people are not extraordinary. This realization is liberating because it helps people accept their ordinary circumstances and find purpose within them.

4. The Value of Suffering

Manson introduces the idea that we all have values that determine how we assess pain and success. Faulty values, like the pursuit of constant pleasure or avoidance of responsibility, lead to more pain. Good values, which are reality-based, socially constructive, and immediate and controllable, lead to a more meaningful existence.

5. The Denial of Responsibility

People often deny responsibility to avoid pain. However, by taking responsibility for our actions and their outcomes, we gain power over our circumstances.

6. The Importance of Uncertainty

Manson emphasizes that it's okay not to know everything. The pursuit of certainty often leads to extreme dogmas and mindsets. Admitting we don't know leads to growth and learning.

7. The Value of Rejection

Instead of avoiding negative experiences or rejections, Manson encourages readers to embrace them. It's through adversity that we learn about ourselves and refine our values.

8. The Power of Death

Manson discusses how the acknowledgment of our mortality can provide clarity and perspective. By recognizing that we're all going to die, we can focus on what truly matters.

Why "The Subtle Art of Not Giving a F*ck" is Significant:

Mark Manson's "The Subtle Art of Not Giving a F*ck" stands out in the realm of self-help literature by challenging the often-superficial positivity permeating the genre. Instead of offering clichéd platitudes, Manson presents a raw, unfiltered perspective on life that resonates with readers seeking authenticity. The book's focus on confronting uncomfortable truths, refining personal values, and accepting the imperfections of life makes it a refreshing guide for those looking to live a life of meaning amidst modern chaos and distractions.

37

"Mindset: The New Psychology of Success" by Carol S. Dweck

In "Mindset: The New Psychology of Success," psychologist Carol S. Dweck explores the concept of "fixed" and "growth" mindsets and how these attitudes influence success and overall potential. The book delves into how one's beliefs about ability impact their behavior, responses to setbacks, and understanding of success.

1. The Two Mindsets
Dweck identifies two primary mindsets that shape our lives:

- **Fixed Mindset:** Those with a fixed mindset believe that abilities and intelligence are static traits that one is born with. They see challenges as threats, tend to avoid effort because it's seen as fruitless, and often give up in the face of obstacles. They feel the need to constantly prove themselves and are threatened by the success of others.
- **Growth Mindset:** Individuals with a growth mindset, on the other hand, believe that abilities can be developed

through dedication and hard work. They see challenges as opportunities to learn and grow, are resilient in the face of setbacks, and believe effort is a pathway to mastery. For them, the journey is as important, if not more so, than the end result.

2. Fixed Mindset in Action

Dweck uses real-life examples to show how a fixed mindset limits achievement and creates an aversion to risk and challenge. Such individuals often plateau early in life and fail to achieve their full potential.

3. Growth Mindset in Action

Contrarily, a growth mindset fosters a passion for learning rather than a hunger for approval. Such individuals continually evolve, learn, and set higher benchmarks for themselves, often achieving more than their fixed mindset counterparts.

4. Mindsets in Love (or Why We're Attracted to Fixed Mindset Partners)

Relationships, Dweck argues, are profoundly affected by our mindsets. Fixed mindset individuals tend to view partners through the lens of judgment (good/bad partner), while those with a growth mindset see partners as collaborators in mutual growth.

5. Parents, Teachers, and Coaches: Where Do Mindsets Come From?

Dweck examines the role of influential figures in developing mindsets during formative years. The feedback and reinforcement from parents, teachers, and coaches can either promote a fixed or growth mindset.

6. Changing Mindsets

While mindsets are deeply held beliefs, they aren't static. Dweck discusses how one can transition from a fixed to a growth mindset, embracing change, seeking challenges, and seeing effort as a journey to learning and growth.

Why "Mindset: The New Psychology of Success" is Significant:

Carol S. Dweck's exploration of the fixed and growth mindsets has had profound implications in various fields, including education, sports, business, and relationships. The book challenges long-held beliefs about talent, potential, and intelligence, suggesting that mindset plays a crucial role in determining success. By highlighting the malleability of mindset, Dweck empowers readers with the understanding that they can change their beliefs and attitudes, leading to greater achievement, resilience, and satisfaction in all areas of life. It's a transformative work that has reshaped the discourse on success and personal potential.

38

"Drive" by Daniel H. Pink

In "Drive," Daniel H. Pink delves into the intricacies of human motivation, challenging traditional views and presenting a revised framework for what drives us in the 21st century. He argues that while our society and workplaces often rely on extrinsic motivators (rewards and punishments), it's the intrinsic motivators that are more powerful and aligned with how we live and work today.

1. The Three Drives

Pink identifies three primary drives of human motivation:

- **Motivation 1.0:** This is our most basic drive – the biological imperative to survive. It's about satisfying our fundamental needs for food, safety, and reproduction.
- **Motivation 2.0:** This is the carrot-and-stick approach, rooted in external rewards and punishments. Pink argues that while this might have been effective during the 20th century, it's not as relevant in the current age, and can even be detrimental to creativity and innovation.

- **Motivation 3.0:** This revolves around the intrinsic motivations that truly drive people — autonomy, mastery, and purpose. Pink asserts that businesses and societies should move towards this form of motivation to unlock higher productivity, satisfaction, and well-being.

2. Autonomy

One of the pillars of Motivation 3.0 is autonomy: the desire to be self-directed. Pink suggests that when people have agency over what they do, when they do it, and who they do it with, they're more engaged and perform better.

3. Mastery

Mastery is the intrinsic desire to get better at something that matters. It's not about being the best, but about constantly improving and honing one's skills. Pink emphasizes that mastery is a mindset: it requires effort, grit, and seeing potential failure as a growth opportunity.

4. Purpose

The third pillar is purpose, which is the yearning to be a part of something larger than oneself. When individuals or organizations align with a genuine purpose, they're more motivated, effective, and fulfilled.

5. The Mismatch of Rewards

While traditional forms of rewards can work for routine tasks, Pink presents evidence that for creative and conceptual tasks — which dominate the modern workplace — these extrinsic rewards can limit performance and stifle creativity.

6. The New Approach to Business Drawing from various examples, Pink highlights businesses and initiatives that have embraced Motivation 3.0, granting employees greater autonomy, fostering environments conducive to mastery, and aligning work with a meaningful purpose.

Why "Drive" is Significant:

Daniel H. Pink's "Drive" offers a revolutionary perspective on motivation in the modern era. By juxtaposing traditional reward systems with the deeper, intrinsic motivators of autonomy, mastery, and purpose, Pink provides a roadmap for individuals and organizations to navigate the challenges of the 21st century. The book, backed by research and punctuated with real-world examples, provides invaluable insights for educators, leaders, and anyone interested in understanding the underlying factors that truly motivate human behavior in today's complex landscape. It's a clarion call for rethinking how we motivate, manage, and engage in the modern world.

39

"Grit: The Power of Passion and Perseverance" by Angela Duckworth: In-Depth Summary

In "Grit," psychologist Angela Duckworth presents a compelling case for the power of passion and perseverance over talent in determining success. Drawing on her own research, as well as insights from various domains, Duckworth explores the nature of grit and its pivotal role in achieving long-term goals.

1. Talent vs. Grit

Duckworth starts by challenging the widespread belief in the supremacy of talent. While talent is important, Duckworth argues that grit—a combination of passion and perseverance—is a more critical determinant of success. A person with average talent but higher grit can outperform a more talented individual with less grit.

2. Effort Counts Twice

Duckworth introduces a formula: Talent x Effort = Skill; Skill x Effort = Achievement. This means effort has a double effect, first in developing skill and then in translating that skill into achievement. Thus, effort plays a crucial role in the journey from potential to real-world success.

3. What Grit Isn't

It's essential to understand what grit is not. Grit isn't just working hard; it's about working consistently towards long-term goals. It's also different from stubbornness, as it involves a deep passion and commitment rather than sheer obstinacy.

4. The Grit Scale

Duckworth introduces the "Grit Scale," a tool she developed to measure one's level of grit. This tool has been used in various settings and consistently demonstrates that higher grit levels correlate with success.

5. Growing Grit from the Inside Out

Duckworth discusses the intrinsic factors that can foster grit:

- **Interest:** Passion begins with a genuine interest. It's essential to cultivate and nurture this interest to develop passion.
- **Practice:** Deliberate practice, which involves focused and repetitive actions with the aim of improvement, is crucial.
- **Purpose:** Connecting personal interests to a larger, external purpose can amplify passion and perseverance.
- **Hope:** The belief that efforts can improve the future is a cornerstone of grit.

6. Growing Grit from the Outside In

External factors can also play a role in nurturing grit:

- **Parenting for Grit:** Supportive yet demanding parenting can foster grit in children.
- **The Playing Fields of Grit:** Activities like sports, which require discipline and resilience, can be breeding grounds for grit.
- **Culture of Grit:** A community or organization's culture can influence the grit of its members.

7. Limitations of Grit

Duckworth acknowledges that grit isn't everything. While it's a significant factor in success, other factors like luck, opportunity, and support play roles. Moreover, it's crucial to ensure that one's gritty pursuit aligns with personal and societal good.

Why "Grit" is Significant:

Angela Duckworth's "Grit" reshapes the discourse on success by emphasizing the qualities of passion and perseverance. By deconstructing myths surrounding talent and providing insights into the cultivation of grit, Duckworth's work offers a fresh perspective on personal achievement. The book provides invaluable lessons for educators, parents, leaders, and anyone striving for long-term goals, making it a cornerstone in the fields of psychology and self-improvement.

40

"The Four Agreements" by Don Miguel Ruiz"

"The Four Agreements" is a spiritual guide by Don Miguel Ruiz that draws on ancient Toltec wisdom to present a code of conduct for achieving personal freedom and a fulfilling life. The book stresses the importance of these four agreements in breaking free from limiting beliefs and societal constructs.

1. Be Impeccable with Your Word
The first agreement emphasizes the power of words. Ruiz argues that one should speak with integrity, say only what one means, and use the power of their words in the direction of truth and love. This involves avoiding gossip, speaking positively about oneself and others, and understanding the profound impact words can have on one's reality.

2. Don't Take Anything Personally
Ruiz suggests that what others say or do is a projection of their own reality and not about you. By not taking things personally, one can avoid needless suffering from others' opinions or

actions. When we become immune to the opinions and actions of others, we won't be the victim of needless suffering.

3. Don't Make Assumptions
To avoid misunderstandings, sadness, and drama, one should not make assumptions. It's essential to have the courage to ask questions and express what you truly want. Ruiz urges readers to communicate as clearly as possible to prevent misinterpretation and to establish an understanding with others.

4. Always Do Your Best
The fourth agreement is about recognizing that "your best" can vary from moment to moment. It urges one to always do their best under any circumstance, which prevents self-judgment, self-abuse, and regret. By ensuring that one is always doing their best, they can maintain self-respect and fulfillment.

5. The Power of the Agreements
Ruiz explains that while these agreements may seem simple, they have profound implications when practiced. They have the potential to transform lives by replacing old, limiting beliefs (which Ruiz calls the "dream of the planet") with a new personal freedom.

6. The Challenge of Living the Agreements
Ruiz acknowledges that living these agreements consistently is challenging due to ingrained patterns and societal conditioning. However, by understanding and practicing the agreements, one can break free from these limitations and achieve a life of freedom, true happiness, and love.

Why "The Four Agreements" is Significant:

Don Miguel Ruiz's "The Four Agreements" offers a transformative roadmap for those seeking spiritual enlightenment, personal freedom, and a deeper understanding of the self. Its simplicity is its strength; the agreements are straightforward yet profound. The book challenges readers to reflect on their deep-seated beliefs, societal conditioning, and daily behaviors. By distilling ancient Toltec wisdom into practical guidelines, Ruiz provides an accessible guide for anyone seeking to lead a life of authenticity, love, and personal freedom. It's a timeless piece that resonates with people across cultures and backgrounds, making it a staple in modern spiritual literature.

41

"You Are a Badass" by Jen Sincero

"You Are a Badass" is a self-help book by Jen Sincero that aims to empower readers to embrace their potential, get rid of self-limiting beliefs, and take control of their lives. Using a blend of humor, personal anecdotes, and actionable advice, Sincero guides readers through a journey of self-discovery and transformation.

1. Embrace Your Inner Badass
Sincero begins by encouraging readers to recognize and embrace their inner "badass" – the authentic self that is deserving of love, success, and happiness. This involves confronting and dispelling negative self-perceptions and understanding one's inherent worth.

2. Self-awareness and Limiting Beliefs
Sincero delves into the importance of self-awareness, urging readers to identify and challenge their limiting beliefs. These beliefs, often formed in childhood or through negative experiences, act as barriers to achieving one's desires.

3. The Power of the Subconscious

The author discusses how the subconscious mind plays a critical role in shaping our reality. By understanding and reprogramming our subconscious beliefs, we can align our mindset with our goals and ambitions.

4. The Universe and Vibrations

Sincero introduces the concept that our energy and vibrations attract similar energies from the universe. Positive thoughts and attitudes tend to draw positive experiences and vice versa. She emphasizes the importance of cultivating an abundance mindset and trusting the universe to manifest one's desires.

5. Taking Risks

One of the key themes of the book is the importance of taking risks and stepping outside one's comfort zone. Sincero argues that growth and transformation often require leaps of faith, even in the face of fear.

6. Money Mindset

Sincero tackles the topic of money, challenging readers to reevaluate their relationship with finances. She stresses the importance of viewing money as a tool for achieving goals rather than as a source of evil or stress.

7. Self-love and Forgiveness

Central to Sincero's message is the idea of self-love. She encourages readers to practice self-care, forgive their past mistakes, and embrace their imperfections.

8. Decision and Action

Ultimately, realizing one's potential requires making decisions and taking action. Sincero pushes readers to commit to their goals, persist through challenges, and continuously take steps towards their desired life.

Why "You Are a Badass" is Significant:

Jen Sincero's "You Are a Badass" stands out in the self-help genre for its candid and humorous approach. While it covers many traditional self-help topics, Sincero's direct and often irreverent tone makes the content relatable and engaging. The book serves as a rallying cry for individuals to stop doubting their worth and start actively pursuing a life they love. With a mix of personal anecdotes, motivational pep talks, and practical advice, "You Are a Badass" has resonated with readers worldwide, inspiring them to embrace their "badassery" and achieve personal and professional success.

42

"The Magic of Thinking Big" by David J. Schwartz

"The Magic of Thinking Big," written by Dr. David J. Schwartz, is a classic self-help book that encourages individuals to think bigger and positively about themselves, their work, and their life to achieve success. Schwartz provides actionable advice on how to overcome fears, nurture a positive mindset, and harness ambition to achieve one's goals.

1. Believe You Can Succeed and You Will
Schwartz begins with the foundational idea that success starts in the mind. He emphasizes that believing in one's capability is the first step toward achieving any goal. Self-belief drives action and persistence.

2. Cure Yourself of Excusitis
Schwartz introduces the concept of "excusitis" - the disease of making excuses. He identifies common excuses people make related to health, intelligence, age, or luck, and provides guidance on overcoming these self-imposed barriers.

3. Build Confidence and Destroy Fear

Fear and lack of confidence are major obstacles to success. Schwartz offers techniques like action-cures-fear and blending confidence-building activities into one's daily routine to bolster self-assurance.

4. Think Big

Central to the book's premise is the idea of thinking big. By elevating one's thinking, an individual can see bigger possibilities, set higher goals, and ultimately achieve more.

5. Think and Dream Creatively

Schwartz advocates for nurturing creativity and open-mindedness. He suggests techniques like brainstorming, being receptive to new ideas, and encouraging an environment of innovative thinking.

6. You Are What You Think You Are

Highlighting the power of perception, Schwartz underscores that how you think about yourself profoundly influences how others perceive you. Carrying oneself confidently and expecting the best sets the stage for positive interactions and opportunities.

7. Manage Your Environment

The environment, including the people and conditions around us, impacts our mindset and actions. Schwartz emphasizes surrounding oneself with positive influences and avoiding negative ones.

8. Turn Defeat into Victory

Setbacks are inevitable, but Schwartz posits that failures can be stepping stones to success. He provides strategies for learning from mistakes and using them as growth opportunities.

9. Think Like a Leader

Schwartz rounds off by discussing the qualities of leadership, including thinking progressively, being open-minded, and motivating others. He suggests that by adopting a leadership mindset, one can inspire and influence others positively.

Why "The Magic of Thinking Big" is Significant:

David J. Schwartz's "The Magic of Thinking Big" remains one of the seminal works in the self-help genre, primarily because of its universal appeal and timeless principles. The book distills complex ideas about self-belief, ambition, and positive thinking into actionable advice. Its core message— that the mind is a powerful tool in shaping one's destiny— has resonated with countless readers since its publication. By blending motivational anecdotes with practical strategies, Schwartz has crafted a guide that has empowered individuals across the world to dream big and actualize their potential.

43

"The Alchemist" by Paulo Coelho

"The Alchemist" is a philosophical book that deals more with spiritual wisdom than with gold. Written by Brazilian author Paulo Coelho, the novel is a beautifully crafted allegory about a young Andalusian shepherd named Santiago who dreams of discovering a treasure located near the Egyptian pyramids.

1. The Dream and the Prophecy

Santiago recurrently dreams of a child telling him to find treasure at the base of the Egyptian pyramids. Deciding to pursue this vision, Santiago meets a fortune-teller who tells him to follow his dream.

2. The King of Salem

On his journey, Santiago encounters Melchizedek, the King of Salem. Melchizedek introduces Santiago to the concept of a 'Personal Legend' or a quest that an individual must pursue to realize the essence of their existence. He speaks about the 'Soul of the World' and emphasizes the importance of understanding omens.

3. The Englishman and the Alchemist

On his way to Egypt, Santiago joins a caravan where he meets an Englishman. The Englishman is in search of the titular Alchemist, who he believes will help him turn lead into gold. Their journey together emphasizes the difference between knowledge acquired from books and that gained from personal experience.

4. Love in the Desert

Santiago falls in love with Fatima, a woman of the desert. While he wishes to stay with her, she encourages him to continue his quest, assuring him that if their love is true, they will be reunited once his journey is complete.

5. Meeting the Alchemist

The Alchemist, upon meeting Santiago, recognizes his pure heart and decides to guide him. He teaches Santiago the ways of alchemy and the understanding that true alchemy is not just about turning metal into gold, but about mastering the Language of the World and recognizing the essential unity of all things.

6. The Ultimate Realization

Upon reaching the pyramids, Santiago is attacked by robbers. One of them, unknowingly, reveals that the treasure Santiago seeks is not in Egypt but back in Spain, buried in the very church where his journey began. Santiago understands that the journey was not about the physical treasure but about understanding himself, the workings of fate, and the journey of life.

7. The Treasure

Returning home, Santiago digs beneath a sycamore tree at the church and discovers a chest of gold coins and jewels—the physical manifestation of his treasure. But the true treasure was the wisdom and experiences he gained on his journey.

Why "The Alchemist" is Significant:

Paulo Coelho's "The Alchemist" resonates profoundly with readers around the globe because of its universal themes. The story isn't just about Santiago's journey to find worldly treasure; it's an allegory of each person's journey to fulfill their destiny and understand their personal legend. The book emphasizes the importance of listening to one's heart, recognizing opportunities, and following dreams. Its blend of mysticism, wisdom, and simplicity has made "The Alchemist" a modern classic, offering valuable insights into the human spirit and the pursuit of one's true path in life.

44

"Emotional Intelligence" by Daniel Goleman

"Emotional Intelligence" by Daniel Goleman, published in 1995, delves into the nature of emotional intelligence (often abbreviated as EQ) and its profound impact on personal and professional success. Goleman posits that EQ can be as important, if not more so, than traditional intelligence (IQ) in predicting life success.

1. The Nature of Emotional Intelligence
Goleman begins by defining emotional intelligence as the ability to recognize, understand, manage, and regulate our emotions and the emotions of others. Unlike IQ, which remains relatively stable throughout life, EQ can be developed and enhanced with practice and intention.

2. The Five Components of EQ
Goleman identifies five key components of emotional intelligence:

- **Self-awareness**: Recognizing and understanding one's emotions.
- **Self-regulation**: Controlling and managing one's emotions, especially negative ones.
- **Motivation**: Being driven to pursue goals for personal reasons rather than external rewards.
- **Empathy**: Understanding and recognizing the emotions of others.
- **Social skills**: Building relationships and interacting harmoniously with others.

3. The Brain and Emotion

Goleman delves into neuroscience to explain the anatomy of an emotional hijack, where rationality gets overshadowed by emotions. He discusses the amygdala's role, a part of the brain vital for emotion, and how it can sometimes override the neocortex, the area responsible for rational thought.

4. Emotional Literacy

The author posits that emotional literacy should be nurtured from a young age. He discusses the value of programs in schools that teach children how to handle conflicts, manage distressing emotions, and be empathetic. Such programs, Goleman argues, have benefits that manifest in better behavior and improved academic performance.

5. The Role of EQ in Personal and Professional Success

Throughout the book, Goleman presents various studies and examples that highlight the importance of emotional intelligence in different areas of life. He suggests that a high EQ can lead to better relationships, career success, and overall well-being. Conversely, a lack of emotional intelligence can lead to a host of personal and societal problems, including aggression, depression, and poor interpersonal relationships.

6. Improving Emotional Intelligence

Goleman concludes by offering hope that emotional intelligence is not a fixed trait. Through self-awareness, mindfulness, and dedication, individuals can enhance their EQ. He provides guidance on how adults can improve their emotional intelligence and underscores the importance of imparting these skills to the next generation.

Why "Emotional Intelligence" is Significant:

Daniel Goleman's "Emotional Intelligence" brought the concept of EQ into the mainstream and challenged the traditionally held belief that IQ alone was the primary determinant of success. The book is groundbreaking in its assertion that emotions, when understood and managed properly, can be a source of strength, providing clarity in decision-making, resilience against setbacks, and the ability to connect with others. By emphasizing the trainable nature of EQ, Goleman's work has had a lasting impact on education, corporate training, and personal development, fostering a more holistic understanding of human intelligence and potential.

45

"Getting Things Done" by David Allen

"Getting Things Done" (often abbreviated as GTD) by David Allen is a comprehensive time and productivity management system that focuses on task organization and completion. Introduced in 2001, Allen's methodology has been adopted by individuals and businesses worldwide. The GTD system is designed to alleviate feelings of overwhelm, enhance focus, and ensure that all tasks, whether big or small, are captured, organized, and actioned.

1. The GTD Workflow
Allen presents a five-stage workflow for processing and managing tasks:

- **Capture**: Collect everything that has your attention. Write down tasks, ideas, projects, and other commitments into an inbox.
- **Clarify**: Process what each item means. Decide if it's actionable. If it is, decide the next action; if not, discard it, defer it, or file it for reference.

- **Organize**: Sort these actions based on their context, urgency, and other criteria. Use lists, calendars, and other tools.
- **Reflect**: Regularly review your system to ensure you're focused on the right tasks. Allen recommends a weekly review to update and prioritize tasks.
- **Engage**: Execute the tasks based on priority and context.

2. The Two-Minute Rule

If a task will take less than two minutes, do it immediately. This principle ensures that small tasks don't pile up and become overwhelming.

3. Context-Based Lists

Allen recommends organizing tasks based on their context, such as @calls (for phone calls to be made), @computer (tasks to be done on a computer), or @errands. This approach allows for batching similar tasks and tackling them when you're in the appropriate setting or mindset.

4. The Importance of a Trusted System

For GTD to work effectively, individuals must fully trust their organizational system. This means regularly capturing all tasks and commitments, keeping the system up-to-date, and consistently reviewing and actioning items.

5. Natural Planning Model

Allen suggests a planning model that mirrors the way people naturally plan:

- **Purpose and Principles**: Define the purpose of your project

and the principles guiding it.
- **Outcome Visioning**: Envision the result you want.
- **Brainstorming**: Generate ideas without judging.
- **Organizing**: Structure your ideas, identifying significant components and priorities.
- **Identifying Next Actions**: Decide the immediate next steps.

6. The Weekly Review

The Weekly Review is a cornerstone of the GTD system. It's a dedicated time to update lists, process inboxes, review upcoming tasks, and ensure alignment with personal and professional goals.

7. Stress-Free Productivity

GTD's overarching goal is "stress-free productivity." By ensuring everything is captured and organized outside of the mind, individuals free up mental space, reduce anxiety over forgotten tasks, and can fully engage with their work or leisure activities.

Why "Getting Things Done" is Significant:

David Allen's "Getting Things Done" addresses the modern challenge of information and task overload. In an age where commitments, communications, and tasks can quickly become overwhelming, the GTD system offers a structured approach to manage everything that demands attention. By emphasizing the importance of capturing all commitments, big or small, and providing a clear framework for actioning them, Allen's methodology aims to enhance productivity, reduce stress, and bring more clarity and control to both work and personal life. Its enduring popularity and wide adoption are testaments to its effectiveness in meeting these goals.

46

"Influence: The Psychology of Persuasion" by Robert B. Cialdini

"Influence: The Psychology of Persuasion" is a seminal book by Dr. Robert B. Cialdini, a renowned psychologist and researcher. Published in 1984, the book delves into the psychology behind why people say "yes" and the underlying factors that drive individuals to be persuaded. Cialdini introduces six fundamental principles or weapons of influence, each grounded in academic research and enriched with relatable examples.

1. Reciprocity
The principle of reciprocity states that people feel an inherent obligation to return favors. When someone does something for us, we naturally want to repay them in some way. This desire can be leveraged in various situations, such as companies giving out free samples or a colleague helping with a task.

2. Commitment and Consistency
Once people commit to something, they're more likely to follow through with it, especially if this commitment is made

publicly. Cialdini explains that people have a deep-seated desire to appear consistent in their actions and decisions. Sales techniques, like getting someone to agree to a small initial request, can often lead to larger commitments in line with the initial agreement.

3. Social Proof
People often look to others to determine appropriate behavior. In situations of uncertainty, the actions of others provide validation. Examples of social proof are abundant, from laugh tracks in sitcoms to testimonials and reviews in advertising. If many others are doing something, individuals are more likely to perceive that action as correct.

4. Authority
People have a tendency to obey authority figures, even if what they're asked to do goes against their personal beliefs or values. Symbols of authority, such as titles, clothing, or expensive cars, can increase the likelihood of compliance. Cialdini discusses the famous Milgram experiment as a stark example of the power of perceived authority.

5. Liking
We're more likely to be persuaded by people we like. Factors that contribute to likability include physical attractiveness, similarity, compliments, and cooperative endeavors. For example, salespeople may try to find common ground with potential customers to increase rapport and likability.

6. Scarcity
Perceived scarcity generates demand. People place higher value

on opportunities when they are less available, driven by the fear of missing out (FOMO). This principle is evident in limited-time offers, exclusive deals, or the selling of rare collectibles.

Why "Influence: The Psychology of Persuasion" is Significant:

Cialdini's "Influence" stands out for its blend of rigorous academic research and accessible real-world examples. It offers invaluable insights for those in marketing, sales, or any profession that requires persuasion. Beyond its professional relevance, the book equips readers with knowledge to recognize and resist manipulative tactics they might encounter in daily life. By understanding the mechanics of persuasion, individuals are better positioned to navigate a world filled with influence attempts, making more informed and autonomous decisions. The book's enduring popularity underscores its profound impact on understanding the subtle art and science of persuasion.

47

"The Art of Happiness" by Dalai Lama

"The Art of Happiness" is a book that encapsulates conversations between the 14th Dalai Lama and psychiatrist Howard C. Cutler on the subject of happiness. Published in 1998, the book delves into the philosophies and principles that the Dalai Lama believes can lead to a happy life. Through a blend of Eastern spiritual beliefs and Western psychological insights, the book offers readers a guide on how to find contentment and joy.

1. The Purpose of Life is Happiness

The Dalai Lama starts with a profound yet simple premise: the purpose of life is to seek happiness. This foundational belief sets the tone for the entire book. He posits that while suffering is a natural part of life, happiness is attainable through inner development and self-reflection.

2. Sources of Happiness

The Dalai Lama and Cutler explore both internal and external sources of happiness. While external factors, like wealth or status, can influence happiness, true contentment arises from internal sources such as compassion, patience, and a calm mind.

3. The Role of Compassion

Compassion and loving-kindness are central to achieving happiness. The Dalai Lama believes that by cultivating a compassionate heart, we can experience genuine happiness and foster it in others.

4. Overcoming Obstacles

The Dalai Lama discusses various emotional and mental obstacles to happiness, such as anger, hatred, and jealousy. He offers insights into how one can transform and overcome these negative emotions, emphasizing the importance of self-awareness and meditation.

5. Dealing with Suffering

Addressing the universal experience of suffering, the Dalai Lama provides a refreshing perspective. He suggests that suffering can be a path to deeper understanding and spiritual growth, especially when approached with acceptance and a broader perspective on life's transient nature.

6. The Role of Religion

While the Dalai Lama is a religious leader in Buddhism, he stresses that one doesn't need to be religious to lead a happy life. Religion can be a path to happiness for many, but the core values essential for happiness, like kindness and tolerance, can be cultivated outside of religious beliefs.

7. Western Perspectives

Dr. Cutler interweaves the Dalai Lama's insights with Western therapeutic practices and psychological research, providing a comprehensive look at the pursuit of happiness across cultures. Cutler's contributions help bridge the gap between Eastern and Western perspectives, making the teachings more accessible to a global audience.

Why "The Art of Happiness" is Significant:

"The Art of Happiness" is more than just a self-help book; it's a melding of Eastern spiritual wisdom with Western psychological insights. The Dalai Lama's profound yet straightforward teachings, combined with Cutler's interpretations, offer readers tangible advice on leading a fulfilled life. In a world where happiness is often equated with material success, the book provides a refreshing perspective, emphasizing inner values, acceptance, and compassion. The universality of its teachings has made "The Art of Happiness" a beloved classic for those seeking deeper meaning and contentment in their lives.

48

"Flow: The Psychology of Optimal Experience" by Mihaly Csikszentmihalyi

In "Flow: The Psychology of Optimal Experience," Mihaly Csikszentmihalyi delves deep into the state of consciousness where individuals feel their best and perform their best — a state he terms as "flow." The book, published in 1990, draws upon decades of research to unpack the nature of this optimal experience, its significance, and ways to achieve it.

1. What is Flow?
Flow is described as a state of total immersion in an activity, where an individual loses awareness of time, self, and external concerns, fully engrossed in the task at hand. It's often referred to as being "in the zone." During flow, people feel a sense of joy, creativity, and total involvement with life.

2. Characteristics of Flow
Several characteristics define the flow experience:

- **Complete Concentration**: Focusing deeply on the task at hand.

- **Loss of Self-Consciousness**: Not being aware of oneself and feeling part of something larger.
- **Transformation of Time**: Not being aware of the passage of time.
- **Clear Goals**: Understanding what needs to be achieved.
- **Immediate Feedback**: Knowing in real-time how well you are doing.
- **Balance Between Skill and Challenge**: The task is neither too easy nor too difficult.
- **Sense of Control**: Feeling in control of the task and one's actions.
- **Intrinsic Reward**: The activity itself is its own reward.

3. Accessing Flow in Everyday Life

While flow is commonly associated with extraordinary experiences or specialized activities, Csikszentmihalyi suggests that flow can be part of ordinary, daily activities. Whether it's work, hobbies, or even mundane tasks, by setting clear goals, seeking feedback, and adjusting challenges to our skill level, we can experience flow more frequently.

4. Flow and Personal Growth

Flow not only leads to happiness and fulfillment but also facilitates personal growth. Engaging in activities that induce flow helps in the development of skills, resilience, and self-confidence.

5. The Role of Culture and Society

Csikszentmihalyi discusses the role of societal values and cultural frameworks in influencing our experiences of flow.

Societies that prioritize materialism and passive leisure might hinder their members' ability to engage in flow experiences compared to societies that value intrinsic rewards, challenges, and growth.

6. Beyond Individual Flow

While much of the book focuses on individual experiences, Csikszentmihalyi also touches upon collective flow. Groups, teams, or even entire organizations can achieve a flow state when they work cohesively towards a shared goal, benefiting from a heightened sense of connection and achievement.

Why "Flow: The Psychology of Optimal Experience" is Significant:

"Flow" fundamentally shifted our understanding of happiness and human potential. Instead of seeing happiness as a passive state or a byproduct of external events, Csikszentmihalyi positions it as an active, accessible experience that individuals can cultivate. The concept of flow resonates widely — from professional athletes to artists to everyday individuals — because it offers a tangible framework for fulfillment and peak performance. By highlighting the conditions and practices that foster flow, the book empowers readers to lead richer, more engaged lives, irrespective of external circumstances. It remains a cornerstone in positive psychology, human development, and performance studies.

49

"Outliers: The Story of Success" by Malcolm Gladwell

In "Outliers: The Story of Success," Malcolm Gladwell delves into the factors that contribute to high levels of success. Published in 2008, the book challenges the conventional wisdom that personal determination and innate talent are the primary drivers of success. Instead, Gladwell posits that external factors, such as culture, family background, opportunities, and even birth dates, play crucial roles in an individual's success trajectory.

1. The 10,000-Hour Rule
One of the most widely discussed concepts from the book is the idea that it takes roughly 10,000 hours of practice to achieve mastery in a particular field. Gladwell uses examples like The Beatles and Bill Gates to illustrate how consistent practice and opportunity intersect to create outstanding achievement.

2. The Matthew Effect
Based on a biblical verse from the book of Matthew, "For who-

ever has will be given more, and they will have an abundance. Whoever does not have, even what they have will be taken from them." Gladwell explains how small initial advantages can snowball over time. An example he gives is of Canadian hockey players, where those born in the earlier months of the year have a slight age advantage when they start playing, leading to more training and opportunities as they grow.

3. The Role of Culture

Cultural legacies play a significant role in shaping success. Gladwell illustrates this through the story of plane crashes, attributing some accidents to specific cultural norms and communication hierarchies. He also discusses the "rice paddies theory" — the idea that hard work and precision required in rice cultivation in certain Asian countries have given students from those backgrounds an advantage in mathematics.

4. The Importance of Family and Upbringing

Gladwell emphasizes the role of family, particularly the socio-economic status and practices of one's parents and grandparents, in influencing success. Opportunities or lack thereof, the values instilled, and even the professions of our ancestors can shape our paths.

5. Opportunity Knocks

Success is also about being in the right place at the right time. Gladwell discusses how access to unique opportunities, combined with individual effort, can lead to outstanding achievement. Bill Gates, for instance, had rare access to a high-powered computer terminal in his school, allowing him to get a head start on programming.

6. The Outliers

The title "Outliers" refers to individuals who lie outside the norm in their level of success. However, Gladwell's exploration reveals that these outliers often owe their achievements to a combination of factors, many of which are external to them and beyond their control.

Why "Outliers: The Story of Success" is Significant:

"Outliers" offers a fresh perspective on success, challenging the rugged individualism that often permeates discussions on achievement. By highlighting the myriad factors, from birth dates to cultural legacies, that can influence an individual's trajectory, Gladwell underscores the importance of community, context, and luck in shaping success. The book prompts readers to reconsider the narratives they hold about their own achievements or the lack thereof and emphasizes the collective responsibility of creating societies where more people have access to opportunities. Its insights continue to influence educators, policymakers, and anyone interested in understanding the complex tapestry of human achievement.

50

"The Compound Effect" by Darren Hardy

"The Compound Effect," written by Darren Hardy, the former publisher of SUCCESS Magazine, is a motivational and practical guide to achieving success in personal and professional life. The central theme of the book is that small, consistent actions, compounded over time, lead to significant results. Hardy emphasizes that while these actions might seem trivial in the short term, their cumulative effect can be transformative.

1. The Power of the Compound Effect

Hardy introduces the concept of the Compound Effect as the principle of reaping significant rewards from a series of small, smart choices. Much like how compound interest works in finance, small actions, done consistently, can lead to dispro-portionally large and beneficial outcomes over time.

2. The Magic of Small Choices

Every decision, no matter how minor it seems, can contribute to the compound effect. Hardy stresses that success is not about making one-off big changes but about consistently making better choices in everyday life.

3. Habits and Momentum
The formation of good habits is central to leveraging the compound effect. Once established, these habits create a momentum that can propel individuals toward their goals with increasing speed. On the flip side, bad habits can similarly compound, leading to negative outcomes.

4. Influences and Associations
Hardy highlights the role of everyday influences in shaping our decisions and behaviors. He advises readers to be mindful of the information they consume and the people they associate with. Being surrounded by positive influences and associations can significantly amplify the compound effect in a beneficial direction.

5. Tracking and Monitoring
One of the practical tools Hardy recommends is tracking one's actions and behaviors. By documenting and reviewing our choices, we become more aware of our patterns and can adjust our actions to align better with our long-term goals.

6. Overcoming Challenges
Every journey has its setbacks. Hardy acknowledges that challenges and obstacles are part of the process. He encourages readers to see these challenges as opportunities for growth and emphasizes the importance of persisting through difficulties to allow the compound effect to work.

7. Living Intentionally

Hardy calls for intentional living — making conscious and deliberate choices that align with one's goals and values. Instead of drifting through life or waiting for big breaks, he advises taking consistent actions, however small, in the desired direction.

Why "The Compound Effect" is Significant:

"The Compound Effect" stands out for its simplicity and practicality. Instead of proposing radical life overhauls or relying on bursts of motivation, Darren Hardy showcases how everyday decisions, made consistently over time, can lead to monumental changes. This message is both empowering and accessible. Readers come away with the understanding that success isn't necessarily about grand gestures or innate talent but about consistency, persistence, and the transformative power of time. The book offers actionable insights for anyone looking to improve their life, career, or relationships, making it a staple in personal development literature.

51

"The Gifts of Imperfection" by Brené Brown

Dr. Brené Brown, a renowned research professor and story-teller, dives deep into the realms of vulnerability, worthiness, and authenticity in "The Gifts of Imperfection." Throughout the book, Brown encourages readers to embrace their imperfections and recognize them as sources of strength and connection rather than markers of inadequacy.

1. Wholehearted Living

At the heart of the book is the concept of "Wholehearted Living" — a way of engaging with the world from a place of worthiness. It involves cultivating the courage, compassion, and connection to wake up in the morning and think, "No matter what gets done and how much is left undone, I am enough."

2. The Ten Guideposts

Brown introduces ten guideposts to help readers cultivate this Wholehearted life. These guideposts are effectively practices to adopt and things to let go of:

- **Authenticity**: Let go of what people think and embrace genuine self-expression.
- **Self-Compassion**: Let go of perfectionism and treat oneself kindly.
- **Resilience**: Let go of numbing behaviors and develop the ability to bounce back from setbacks.
- **Gratitude and Joy**: Let go of scarcity and fear of the dark, embracing moments of joy with gratitude.
- **Intuition and Trusting Faith**: Let go of the need for certainty.
- **Creativity**: Let go of comparison and dare to create without fear.
- **Play and Rest**: Let go of exhaustion as a status symbol and embrace relaxation and play.
- **Calm and Stillness**: Let go of anxiety and cultivate moments of quiet.
- **Meaningful Work**: Let go of self-doubt and believe that one is enough to make a difference.
- **Laughter, Song, and Dance**: Let go of being cool and in control, embracing the freedom of self-expression.

3. The Role of Shame and Fear

Brown delves deep into the powerful emotions of shame and fear, discussing how they can prevent us from living authentically and wholeheartedly. She emphasizes the importance of understanding and addressing these emotions to cultivate a more fulfilling life.

4. The Power of Connection

Connection with others, Brown argues, is essential for a meaningful life. By accepting our vulnerabilities and imperfections, we can forge deeper connections with others and cultivate genuine belonging.

5. Dig Deep

Brown introduces the "DIG Deep" method: Get **D**eliberate in thoughts and behaviors, get **I**nspired to take action, and get **G**oing when faced with obstacles.

Why "The Gifts of Imperfection" is Significant:

"The Gifts of Imperfection" stands out in the self-help landscape for its grounded approach to embracing vulnerability and imperfection. Brown's research-driven insights, combined with her engaging storytelling, make complex emotional landscapes accessible and relatable. The book offers readers a path to more genuine, connected, and fulfilling lives, challenging societal norms that equate vulnerability with weakness. By emphasizing the value of authenticity, self-compassion, and resilience, Brown provides a blueprint for embracing oneself fully, flaws and all, making "The Gifts of Imperfection" a transformative read in personal development literature.

52

Journey's End and a New Beginning: The Power of Self-Reflection

As we close this enlightening journey through some of the most impactful self-help books ever written, it is essential to remember that the path to self-improvement is never linear, nor does it truly end. Each of these books, from Duhigg's exploration of habits to Brown's insights into vulnerability, has offered unique tools and perspectives to empower individuals in their personal and professional lives.

But the power of these books is not just in their individual messages; it's in the way their ideas interweave, reinforcing and complementing one another. The interconnectedness of these principles is a testament to the universal search for understanding, purpose, and growth that binds humanity together.

Reflect on the Journey

As you step forth, equipped with a treasure trove of wisdom from some of the world's most insightful minds, take a moment to reflect:

- **Revisit the Beginning**: Think back to why you embarked on this journey. What were you seeking? Has that changed during this expedition through the world of self-help?
- **Connect the Dots**: How do the teachings from one book interact with another? For instance, how does the power of habit formation connect with the grit to see things through?
- **Personal Growth**: Celebrate your growth and newfound knowledge. Recognizing and appreciating progress, no matter how small, is vital.

Incorporate What Resonates

Every reader will resonate differently with each book. What's most important is to:

- **Find Your Truths**: Among the myriad principles and guide-lines, determine what genuinely resonates with your beliefs and circumstances.
- **Integrate Gradually**: Rome wasn't built in a day. Incorpo-rate these teachings gradually into your life, giving each one the time it needs to manifest its benefits.

Continual Learning

While this book has encapsulated the essence of fifty renowned self-help books, the world of knowledge is boundless. New perspectives, ideas, and research continually emerge. Keep an open mind:

- **Stay Curious**: Always be on the lookout for new knowledge. Books, seminars, podcasts, and even everyday conversations can be goldmines of insight.
- **Teach and Learn**: Share what you've learned. Teaching not only reinforces your understanding but can also offer others the tools they need on their journey.

Final Thoughts

Your engagement with these summaries is the first step in a transformative journey. The knowledge you've gleaned serves as a foundation upon which you can build a life of purpose, happiness, and fulfillment. Remember, the quest for self-improvement is an ongoing one. As the Japanese principle of *Kaizen* teaches us, continuous improvement, however incremental, leads to substantial long-term growth.

And so, while this chapter marks the end of this book, let it be the prologue to the next chapter in your unique journey of self-discovery and growth. Embrace the future with an open heart, an eager mind, and the invaluable wisdom from some of the best that self-help literature has to offer.

"The journey of a thousand miles begins with one step." — Lao

Tzu

Printed in Great Britain
by Amazon